# Kathmandu & the Kingdom of Nepal

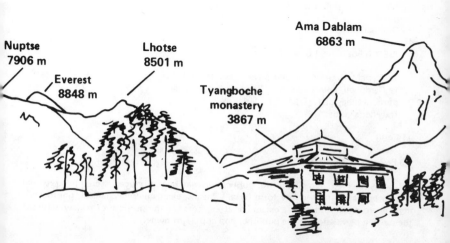

Nuptse
7906 m

Everest
8848 m

Lhotse
8501 m

Tyangboche
monastery
3867 m

Ama Dablam
6863 m

**Kathmandu & the Kingdom of Nepal**

**Published by:**
Lonely Planet Publications
PO Box 88, South Yarra
Victoria 3141, Australia

**Printed in:**
Hong Kong

**Typeset by:**
Affairs Computer Typesetting

**Illustrations by:**
Peter Campbell

**Photographs by:**
Tony Wheeler

**This Edition:**
May 1978


National Library of Australia
Cataloguing in Publication data
Raj, Prakash A., 1943 —.
    Kathmandu & the Kingdom of Nepal

    Index
    First edition published as: Nepal — a traveller's
    guide.
    Bibliography.

    ISBN 0 908086 01 6.

    1. Nepal — Description and travel — Guide-books.
    I. Campbell, Peter, illus. II. Wheeler, Anthony Ian,
    photographer. III. Title. IV. Title: Nepal — a
    traveller's guide.

915.496

© Prakash A Raj 1976, 1978

## And a word from the author

This guide began in 1972, I was just back from Europe where I had used a guide which had given me much information on enjoying Europe with little money to spend. "If I could write a similar guide to Nepal it would be really helpful", I thought. But I wanted to be different to other guides and it struck me that one of the best ways to collect information would be to interview visitors and ask them what they would like to see in a guide on Nepal. I requested them specifically to write a few lines on something special they had found in the country which they could pass on to others.

The first edition of this book was published in Nepal in 1973 and was entitled *Nepal on $2 a Day*. I continued to meet western tourists and ask them for information which I used to revise the book in 1975. When the third edition, published by Lonely Planet Publications, emerged in late 1976 I had interviewed more than 1000 visitors. I have updated all the information for this fourth edition.

In a country changing as fast as Nepal I realise that many things, especially prices, will have altered from how I describe them here. If readers could write to me I will try to make timely corrections in the next edition.

*Prakash A Raj*
*PO Box 941*
*Kathmandu, Nepal*

## DISTRIBUTION

If you can't find Lonely Planet travel guides at your local bookshop or from one of our distributors below please write to us directly in Australia.

| | |
|---|---|
| Hong Kong | Hong Kong University Press<br>94 Bonham Road, Hong Kong |
| India | — New Book Depot, Connaught Place, New Delhi<br>— UBS Distributors, 5 Ansari Rd, New Delhi<br>— Karachi Stationery Mart, 46 Janpath, New Delhi |
| Malaysia | see Singapore |
| Nepal | see India |
| Netherlands | Nilsonn & Lamm bv<br>Pampuslan 212, Weesp, Postbus 195 |
| New Zealand | Caveman Press<br>Box 1458, Dunedin |
| Papua New Guinea | Robert Brown & Associates<br>Box 3395, Port Moresby |
| Philippines | see Singapore |
| Singapore | Apa Productions<br>Room 1021, International Plaza, Anson Rd |
| Thailand | Chalermnit Bookshop<br>1-2 Erawan Arcade, Bangkok |
| UK | Roger Lascelles<br>16 Holland Park Gardens, London W14 8DY |
| USA | Bookpeople<br>2940 Seventh St, Berkeley, California 94710 |

# Contents

# Why Nepal?

The number of travellers who are tired of travelling to the conventional, tourist infested resorts increases year by year. Especially amongst young people there is a genuine yearning for a place which is really different, where the rhythm of life is not that fast, where the way of life is older and less altered by the modern world. Amongst young people Nepal has almost become a legend.

After visiting Kathmandu recently a French writer said:

> . . . the traveller starts to realise that the travel agencies have not told him everything. Some have talked of Kathmandu as being situated in the shadow of Everest (which is not true), others have described it as the Mecca of the hippies (which is only half true), but the most important thing has been left unsaid. It has been forgotten to mention that Kathmandu is the Florence of Asia, the city of art par excellence, a wonder of the modern world where Europe of the middle ages can still be discovered.

Perhaps that is why the number of tourists to Nepal is increasing so dramatically.

Nepal has many other things to offer to a visitor, such as its unique combination of works of man and nature. The flourishing of art and architecture is amply demonstrated by the temples of the Kathmandu Valley; the beauties of nature by soaring peaks like Mount Everest and others lesser in height but even more spectacular in appearance.

Nepal is one of the best places in the world for trekking. Not only is trekking comparatively safe but in remote villages every household would consider it its duty to extend hospitality to a weary traveller. Nor are there many countries in the world where the contrast between old and new is so striking. In the streets of Kathmandu you will see the latest model Japanese cars while only a few minutes away from the capital people cultivate their fields with bullocks. For them things have changed very little in the past five centuries.

The Kathmandu Valley has been called one big museum — a vast storehouse of Hindu and Buddhist art with more shrines and temples per square km than anywhere else in the world. Two hundred years ago, in a statement that has a wisp of truth in it even today, the English author Kirkpatrick said:

> The valley consists of as many temples as there are houses and as many idols as there are men.

Nor is this a dry, dead museum — Nepal celebrates countless festivals every year and has developed institutions such as the *living goddess* to ensure this is a live museum. The Nepalese even boast of having developed the pagoda style of architecture and successfully exported it to China and Japan.

Nepal also contains an amazing mixture of ethnic and racial groups. In the streets of Kathmandu one might think passers by were Japanese, Chinese, Indonesian, Indian, Arab, Greek or Latin American but it is entirely within the bounds of possibility that they would all be Nepalese. Nepal is the only Hindu kingdom in the world but both Hinduism and Buddhism have co-existed amicably for centuries and many people profess both religions. Nepal has never suffered bloodshed in the name of religion. Buddha's birthplace is in Nepal and one of the largest Buddhist stupas in the world can also be found here.

Nepal is one of the few windows looking on to Tibetan life and culture. Tibetan refugees live in many parts of Nepal and run some excellent restaurants and curio shops in Kathmandu. Near the Chinese border some Nepalese also speak Tibetan.

In terms of per capita income, just $US100 in 1974, Nepal is one of the least developed countries in the world. It was also, until 1973, one of the few countries where the smoking of hashish was tolerated — some would even say legal. This was one of the reasons Nepal gained a name as a hippie paradise. Overland travellers consider Kathmandu, with its abundant and varied supply of restaurants, the best place to eat east of Istanbul. As a place to get away from it all and relax at the end of a long trip it can hardly be surpassed. Nor can there be many places in the east where you will run into so many visitors from so many different countries in so small an area.

Nepal is a tiny country, sandwiched between the two largest, in terms of population, countries in the world — India and China. Perhaps as a result of this it has managed to get substantial foreign aid from the USA, USSR, China, India, the UK, West Germany, Switzerland and Israel to name just a few. The east-west road running the length of Nepal through the southern jungle is divided into sections constructed with assistance from India, the USSR, the UK and the Asian Development Bank. China and India have each aided the construction of roads linking Kathmandu with their respective frontiers. India, China and the USSR have each built power generating plants while the Swiss have helped in the rehabilitation of Tibetan refugees and the setting up of a cheese factory, the Germans in the restoration of ancient temples, the Russians have set up a cigarette factory and the Chinese a leather factory. Within walking distance of each other in Kathmandu are libraries opened by the Americans, British, French, Indians, Russian and Chinese.

Nepal is undoubtedly a land of contrasts but evidence suggests this Shangri La is changing fast. In 1976 there were 86,000 tourists compared to just 6,200 in 1961 — visit Nepal soon, before it is too late.

# Facts for the Traveller

## VISAS

Nepal has embassies or consular offices in most European countries, the USA and in most of its Asian neighbours. Overland travellers generally collect their Nepalese visas in Bangkok or Calcutta if west-bound, in New Delhi if travelling east.

Visas cost $US5 or equivalent and are valid for thirty days. Further extensions, up to a maximum of three months, cost Rs 10 for one week or Rs 30 for one month. When extending visas it is necessary to provide proof of official currency exchange of $US5 for each day of the extension — a thirty-day extension thus requires $US150 of exchange. A seven-day visa is available on arrival at Kathmandu airport or at any of the border entry points. This is not advisable for the budget traveller (who will find living at the rate of $US5 per day can actually be difficult!) since he will have to spend much more money for the whole period of his stay in order to extend his visa.

The immigration office (tel 12336) at Ramshah Path extends visas and also issues trekking permits. Local police offices can also extend visas for up to seven days at a time. Nepalese visas are endorsed that they are valid only in and around the Kathmandu and Pokhara Valleys and at Chitwan — Tiger Tops. This does permit travel along all the major roads and short treks around the valley. If you intend to take a longer trek you must obtain a trekking permit for the route you intend to walk. Trekking permits are only available in Kathmandu and can only be extended there.

It is possible to get visas for longer than three months by studying, teaching or undertaking research work at the university or any institution recognised by the government. Many foreigners go to India after the expiry of the three month period, obtain a new one month visa at the Nepalese Embassy and then re-enter Nepal.

If travelling to India after Nepal, visas are not required for Commonwealth citizens or nationals of a number of European countries nor are they required if you arrive in India by air and have outward ticketing within 21 days. This concession does not apply if you are entering India by road and would normally need a visa.

Some of the main Nepalese embassies and consulates abroad are listed below. After a two year gap without representation in Australia a new honorary consul has been appointed and the consulate will be in operation from early 1978.

| | |
|---|---|
| Australia | — PO Box 54, Mosman 2088, Sydney (tel 02-960-1677) |
| France | — 7 Rue Dufrenoy, Paris 16 ( tel 504-6238) |
| West Germany | — 53, Bad Godesberg im Haag 15 (tel 34-3097) |

| | |
|---|---|
| India | — Barakhamba Rd, New Delhi (tel 38-1484) |
| | — 19 Woodlands, Sterndale Rd, Alipore, Calcutta (tel 45-2024) |
| Japan | — 16-3 23 Higashi Gotunda 3, Chome Shinagawa ku Tokyo |
| | (tel 444-7303) |
| Thailand | — 189 Soi Puenguk Sukhumvit 71, Bangkok (tel 391-7240) |
| UK | — 12A Kensington Palace Gardens, London W8 (tel 229-6231) |
| USA | — 2131 Leroy Place, Washington DC 20008 (tel 667-4550) |
| Nepalese Mission to the UN | — 711 3rd Ave, Room 1806, New York 10017 |
| | (tel 986-1989) |

## Other Paperwork

An international driving permit is worth having if there is any chance you
may be driving. Experienced budget travellers do not need to be told how
useful an International Student Identity Card can be — if you can get one do.
If you are youth hostelling then YHA membership may be worth having —
there is a youth hostel in Patan in the Kathmandu valley, if you are travelling
elsewhere in the region you'll find many in India and in south-east Asia. It's
always worth carrying a stack of photos for visa applications, trekking
permits and so on. You won't find western style coin-in-the-slot photo
booths in Nepal of course but Kathmandu's photo studios will do good
quality passport photos at way below western prices. Health insurance is a
wise investment, if you take out trekking insurance make sure it covers
helicopter rescue services as well — being flown out by helicopter is not
cheap!

## HEALTH

A number of vaccinations are highly advisable both for your own safety
and for regulations governing return to your own country although they
may not all be required for entry to Nepal. Diseases to avoid include:

**Smallpox:** Vaccination lasts three years but if your current
immunisation is getting old re-vaccination is a good idea, just a painless
scratch.

**Cholera:** Another important immunisation, usually given as two
injections spaced two weeks apart and valid for six months.

**Typhoid and Paratyphoid:** Also highly recommended, this can be given
with the cholera shot as TAB.

**Tetanus:** Since the TAB shot can also immunise against tetanus as
TABT, this is a worthwhile extra protection.

**Malaria:** Particularly if you are visiting the Terai during the wet season malarial prophylactics are advisable. The usual procedure is a weekly chloroquine tablet or a daily dose of paludrine. In either case start taking the tablets before you arrive in Nepal and continue for two weeks after departure. Malaria has been virtually eradicated from the low lying Terai but care is still advisable.

**Hepatitis:** The best protection against this infectious disease is to take care to eat and drink clean food. Gamma globulin injections have a limited and doubtful efficacy and should be taken as close as possible to your departure time.

Your doctor will record immunisations in your International Certificate of Vaccination which must then be stamped by your local health department. With a little care there is no reason for anyone to catch anything in Nepal. Nepalese pharmacies stock a reasonable range of western pharmaceuticals including aspirin (useful for high altitude headaches if trekking) and cough syrup (often necessary in the cold dry winter air).

## MEDICAL FACILITIES

The government hospital in Kathmandu, known as the *Bir Hospital* (tel. 11119), is modern and does cholera and typhoid vaccinations and issues international health cards. Most westerners needing hospital treatment in Kathmandu go to the *Santa Bhawan Mission Hospital* (tel. 21034) which is across the river in Patan. The out patient service is from 8 to 11 in the morning except Sundays. There is also a good mission hospital in Pokhara — the *Shining Mission Hospital.*

There is a Japanese-trained Nepalese dentist named Dr Mesh Bahadur (tel 12282) just behind the fire station in New Road, clinic hours at 5 to 7 pm. Dr S. K. Pahadi (tel 12331) is a general practitioner with a clinic in the same compound as the Nepal Bank, close to New Road. The clinic of Dr L. N. Prasad (tel 11801), eye, ear, nose and throat specialist, is near the National Theatre. Gamma globulin shots can be obtained at the Kalimati Clinic (tel 14743) for Rs 65.

## CLIMATE AND WHEN TO VISIT

October—November and February—March—April are the best times to visit Nepal. In October and November the weather is excellent, neither too hot nor too cold. As it is immediately after the monsoon there are no clouds or dust in the atmosphere and visibility is extremely good, the Himalayan range will be clearly visible. Rice is harvested in Nepal during these months and two of the biggest festivals also take place — the Nepalese people will be in a happy and festive mood. This is also the best time for trekking.

In the February to April period the weather is still excellent but due to dust in the air visibility is not quite so good. On the other hand if you go trekking you can see the blooming of flowers at high altitude, especially Nepal's brilliant rhododendrons. The weather in mid winter, December and January, is still fine and clear but it can be quite cool especially at high altitude where nights can be exceedingly bitter.

The monsoon lasts from the second week of June to the first week of October and this is not the best time to visit the country — although it will be cool and pleasant compared to the plains of India. Trekking is impossible during this season as the trails are slippery and difficult to walk on, rivers may be impassable and Nepal's horrendous leeches will be out waiting for you. Roads can also be blocked at this time due to landslides and the Himalayan peaks are rarely visible due to the constant cloud cover.

If you visit Nepal in this period a one-week stay in Kathmandu should be adequate with just a short visit out of the valley. If you come in the dry season from October to June a two to four week stay is better. A week can easily be spent in and around the Kathmandu Valley followed by a week's stay in Pokhara including a short trek. If you have time a ten day trek can be made to Ghodepani or Ghandruk from Pokhara or to Helambu from Kathmandu. The long trek to the Everest base camp can even be squeezed into two weeks if you fly back to Kathmandu from Lukla.

Maximum summer temperatures in Kathmandu approach 30°C and even at the height of winter a daily maximum approaching 20°C can be expected. Night temperatures in mid winter can fall to nearly freezing point, 0°C, but it never actually snows in the valley. Pokhara is generally somewhat hotter due to its lower altitude. Nepal's great altitude variations make for some considerable climatic variations from the summer heat on the lowland Terai to the intense cold of the high Himalayas in winter. The Himalayas in Nepal are about 1500 km nearer to the equator than the European Alps — one of the reasons the snow line is so much higher. Apart from the brief winter monsoon, lasting just a day or two in late January, all the rain falls during the monsoon. The lack of precipitation in the winter is another reason for the high snow line, the mountains usually have more snow during the summer.

## MONEY

The Nepalese unit of currency is the Rupee which is divided into 100 paisa. There are approximately 12.5 Nepalese Rupees to the US dollar.

Indian and Nepalese Rupees are freely convertible and 100 Indian Rs equals 139 Nepalese Rs. At the time of going to press the official exchange rates in Nepal were:

| | |
|---|---|
| 1 US Dollar | 12.45 Rs |
| 100 Indian Rupees | 139 Rs |
| 1 German Mark | 5.52 Rs |
| 1 French Franc | 2.55 Rs |
| 1 Sterling Pound | 22.54 Rs |
| 1 Australian Dollar | 13.91 Rs |
| 1 Canadian Dollar | 11.15 Rs |
| 1 Swiss Franc | 5.31 Rs |
| 1 Swedish Kroner | 2.57 Rs |
| 1991 Japanese Yen | 100 Rs |
| 7124 Italian Lira | 100 Rs |
| 130 Austrian Schillings | 100 Rs |

Nepalese currency consists of:
    Coins of 5, 10, 25, 50 paisa
    Banknotes of 1, 5, 10, 50, 100, 500, 1000 rupees

Garuda on Rs 10 note

Kathmandu's two banks are the Rashtriya Bank with an exchange office at New Road Gate, open from 8 am to 8 pm, and the Nepal Bank also on New Road with an exchange counter open 10 am to 2 pm Sunday to Thursdays and 10 am to 12 pm on Friday. The Rashtriya Bank also has an exchange office in the Thamel area of Kathmandu. Most major travellers cheques can be exchanged at these offices or, usually for resident guests only, at major hotels. Unlike many countries the exchange rate in hotels is identical to the banks. It is wise to get some of your money in smaller Rupee denominations. The Rs 100 notes may be difficult to change, particularly in the hills if you go trekking.

Upon entry to Nepal visitors are given a currency exchange card which they are advised to have filled and stamped each time they change money or travellers cheques. When leaving the country you can re-exchange Nepalese currency providing the amount does not exceed 10% of the total changed or the last amount exchanged — whichever is greater. There is an exchange counter in the international terminal of the airport.

There is a bank office in Pokhara and money changers operate at border points such as Birganj. Elsewhere in the country you could expect to have difficulty changing travellers cheques although US dollars can still be changed in major towns. It is advisable to carry sufficient Nepalese currency when trekking to last the whole trek. Until comparatively recently paper money was almost unknown outside the Kathmandu Valley. Mountaineering expeditions in the fifties would have to have several porters simply to carry the operating money for the expedition and porters' wages — in coins! Several books on expeditions through Nepal speak of the proud swagger of the porter entrusted with carrying half his weight in cash.

## GENERAL INFORMATION

### Working Days

Saturday is an inauspicious day and most shops and all offices and banks will be closed — Sunday is a regular working day.

### Time

Nepalese time is 5 hr 40 min ahead of GMT, noon in London is 5.40 pm in Kathmandu. The odd ten minutes is intended to differentiate Nepal from India which is 5 hr 30 min ahead of GMT.

### What to Wear

During most of the year light summer clothes are all you'll need in Kathmandu and the valley. An umbrella is a vital addition during the monsoon and in the depths of winter you'll want a sweater during the day and a warm coat at night. In the mountains, even in mid winter, the days will be warm but the nights bitterly cold. The burning power of the sun at high altitudes is phenomenal — sunglasses and covering unprotected skin are advisable.

### Film and Camera

Although Kathmandu has a number of camera shops obtaining film is both expensive and difficult. What film there is available has usually been sold by visitors and is of doubtful age and quality. If you are using an SLR camera a telephoto lens is a virtual necessity for good mountain close-ups when trekking. Remember also to allow for the exceptional intensity of mountain light when setting exposures at high altitude. Most Nepalese people are quite happy to be photographed but they may demand baksheesh for posing. Sherpa people are an exception and can be very camera shy.

## Electricity

Electric current, when available, is 220 volts/50 cycles throughout Nepal — American 120 volt electrical items will require a transformer.

## Tipping

Tipping is not a normal practise in Nepal so please don't make it one. Taxi drivers certainly don't expect to be tipped nor do budget hotels and restaurants. Only in the more expensive establishments will there be a 10% service charge added to your bill.

## Police

The police phone number is 11999.

## Airline Offices   * Fly to Nepal

Air France, Annapurna Hotel Arcade, Durbar Marg (tel 13339)
Air India, Ratna Park, Kantipath (tel 12335)
Bangladesh Biman*, Durbar Marg (tel 21544)
British Airways, Durbar Marg (tel 12266)
Burma Airways Corporation*, Durbar Marg (tel 14839)
Indian Airlines*, Ranipokhari (tel 11196)
Japan Airlines, Trans Himalayan Trekking, Durbar Marg (tel 13854)
KLM, Gorkha Travels, Durbar Marg (tel 14896)
Lufthansa, Annapurna Hotel Arcade, Durbar Marg (tel 13052)
Pakistan International Airlines, Durbar Marg (tel 12102)
Pan American, Durbar Marg (tel 15824)
Royal Nepal Airlines*, New Road (tel 14511)
SAS, c/o Thai International
Thai International*, Annapurna Hotel Arcade, Durbar Marg (tel 14387 & 13565)
TWA, Kanti Path (tel 14704)

## Postal Services

The Kàthmandu *GPO* is on the corner of Kantipath and Khichapokhari close to the Bhimsen Tower and opens from 10 am to 5 pm daily; a small stamp counter opens earlier. There is a separate *International Post Office* for parcels and a *Telecommunications Office* both situated quite close to the *GPO*. The Poste Restante counter is in the *GPO* and is quite efficient but as anywhere in Asia you are advised to ask that your surname is printed clearly and underlined if you are having mail sent to the Poste Restante. There is also a post office counter at the airport.

## Postal Rates

| | |
|---|---|
| Aerogrammes | Rs 1.50 |
| Air mail postcards | 1.75 |
| Air mail to 20 gm — | |
|     Africa, Europe | 3.50 |
|     Australia, USA | 4.00 |
| Registration | 2.00 |

## Government Offices

Immigration and other government offices are open from 10 am to 5 pm from Sunday to Friday and from 10 am to 4 pm during three winter months.

## Government Tourist Office

The tourist office on Ganga Path by the Basantapur Square (tel 11293) has a large variety of brochures and maps and shows films on Nepal.

## Travel Agencies

Annapurna Travels, Durbar Marg (tel 13940)
Continental Travels & Tours, Durbar Marg (tel 14299)
Dolkha Travels & Tours, Kantipath (tel 15392)
Everest Travel Service, New Road — Basantapur Square (tel 11216)
Gorkha Travels, Durbar Marg (tel 14895)
Himalayan Travels & Tours, Durbar Marg, Ranipokhari (tel 11682)
International Travels (tel 12635)
Kathmandu Tours & Travels, Dharma Path — New Road (tel 14446)
Natraj Travels & Tours, Ghantaphar (tel 12014)
President Travel & Tours, Durbar Marg (tel 15021)
Pokhara Tours & Travel, New Road (tel 14613)
Shankar Travels & Tours, Shankar Hotel, Lazimpat (tel 13494)
Third Eye Travels, Kantipath (tel 11738)
Trans Himalayan Tours, Durbar Marg (tel 13871)
Universal Tours & Travel, Kantipath (tel 12080)
Yak Travel & Tours, Durbar Marg (tel 15611)
Yeti Travels, Durbar Marg (tel 12329 & 11234)

## Foreign Embassies

Bangladesh, Kalikasthan (tel 13509)
Burma, Panipokhari, Maharajganj (tel 13146)
Democratic Republic of Korea, Lainchaur (tel 13567)
Egypt, Ram Shah Path (tel 12945)
Federal Republic of Germany, Kantipath (tel 11730)
France, Lazimpat (tel 12332)
German Democratic Republic, Tripureshwar (tel 14801)
Great Britain, Lainchaur (tel 11588)
India, Lainchaur (tel 11300)
Israel, Bishramalaya-Lazimpat (tel 11251)
Italy, Durbar Marg (tel 12743)
Japan, Lazimpat (tel 13264)
Libya, Dillibazar (tel 12103)
Pakistan, Panipokhari (tel 11431)
People's Republic of China, Toran Bhawan, Naxal (tel 11289)
Poland, Kalikasthan (tel 12694)
Republic of Korea, Thamel (tel 11172)
Thailand, Jyoti Kendra Building, Thapathali (tel 13912)
USA, Ranipokhari-Maharjganj (tel 12718)
USSR, Dillibazar (tel 11255)

# Facts about the Country

## HISTORY

In the course of history the area of Nepal has shrunk and expanded. Sometimes it consisted only of Kathmandu and neighbouring principalities; at other times it extended further east and west from its present boundaries. Nepal's history is a long one, a stone pillar erected more than 2000 years ago by the Indian emperor Ashoka at Lumbini in southern Nepal marks it as the birthplace of Buddha. During those 2000 years Nepal has seen a steady migration of people speaking Indo-European languages from the western Himalayas and the plains of India on one hand and Mongoloid people speaking Tibeto-Burmese languages from Tibet on the other.

The first known rulers of the Kathmandu Valley were the Kirats who had come from the eastern part of the country. Little is known about these people but one of their kings did rate a mention in the *Mahabharata* and it was at this time that Buddhism arrived in the country. Lichhavis came to power from north India during the 4th century AD to the early 7th century, again comparatively little is known about them but at the temple of Changu Narayan a stone inscription can be seen dating from this period.

During the 17th century the three independent, sovereign kingdoms of the Malla dynasty in the Kathmandu Valley created great numbers of works of art, statues and temples. The kingdoms minted their own coins and maintained standing armies. At this time all Nepal was divided into small principalities and kingdoms, western Nepal alone had twenty two and there were a further twenty four in far western Nepal.

From one of these small kingdoms, Gorkha where kings of the Shah dynasty ruled, King Prithvi Narayan Shah set out to unify Nepal. In 1768 he defeated the Malla Kings and Nepal has been ruled by Shah Kings ever since. For half a century after 1768 Nepal continued to extend boundaries until in 1817 Nepal lost a war with Britain. As reward for its support during the Indian Mutiny Nepal regained part of its lost territory in 1858 and assumed its present size.

In 1846 Jung Bahadur, Prime Minister of Nepal, took over real power, after the *Kot massacre* where his supporters managed to kill almost all his opponents, and for over a century the hereditary family of *Rana* Prime Ministers ruled the country and did very little for development. While almost all the countries of Asia and Africa were being colonised Nepal managed to preserve its independence and was never ruled by a colonial power. Throughout the Rana period Nepal was virtually isolated from the rest of the world, visitors were rarely admitted and then only with severely circumscribed freedom of movement. In 1951 King Tribhuvan overthrew the Rana regime with support from India, it was in many ways a unique situation as a king had led a revolution against an oligarchic system. King Tribhuvan died in 1955 and was succeeded by his son King Mahendra, father of the present king.

Nepal became a member of the United Nations in 1955 and was even elected a member of the Security Council for a two year period in 1969-1970. After a decade of experiments in parliamentary democracy, including elections for parliament in 1958, King Mahendra introduced a system of partyless *Panchayat* democracy in 1962. King Birendra ascended the throne after his father's death in 1972 but his coronation did not take place until an auspicious date in February 1975, three years later, had been selected by astrologers. Many foreign dignitaries attended the colourful coronation ceremony in the historic old royal palace.

King Birenda was educated at Eton in England and Harvard in the US. He is intensely interested in the development of Nepal and the country has made significant progress under his leadership. Nepal has been divided into four development regions: Pokhara (western Nepal), Surkhet (Far Western Nepal) and Dhankuta (eastern Nepal) are the regional development centres away from Kathmandu.

## GEOGRAPHY, POPULATION AND ECONOMY

Although Nepal is a small country of only 141,577 sq km it contains the greatest altitude variation on earth from the lowland Terai almost at sea level to Mt Everest which at 8848 m is the highest point on earth. The country is about 800 km long and from 90 to 230 km wide. A cross section shows four main areas to the country. Closest to the border with India is a low fertile strip of jungle land known as the Terai. Until comparatively recently malaria made this an inhospitable region but its eradication has led to a rapid population increase.

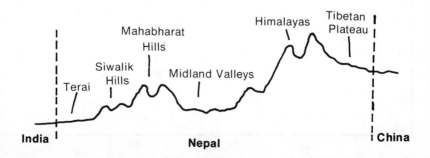

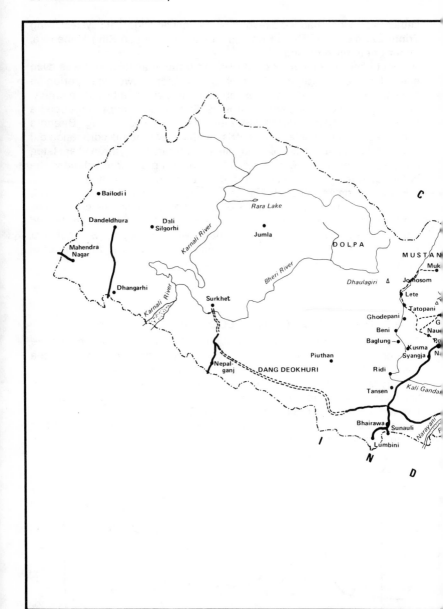

# Nepal

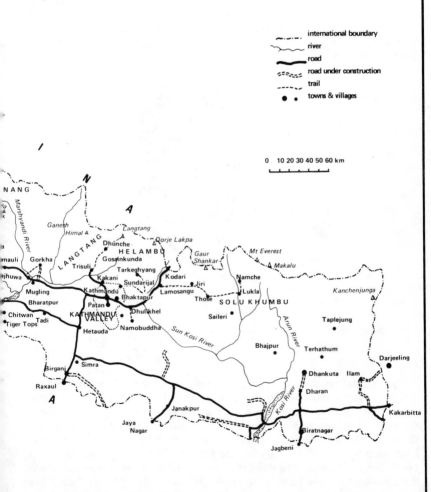

international boundary
river
road
road under construction
trail
towns & villages

0  10 20 30 40 50 60 km

NANG

Marshyandi River

N

A

Ganesh Himal

Langtang

LANGTANG

Dorje Lakpa

mauli  Gorkha

Dhunche

HELAMBU

Gaur Shankar

Mt Everest

Trisuli

Gosainkunda

Makalu

jhuwa

Kakani

Tarkeghyang

Kodari

Namche

Mugling

Sundarijal

Lamosangu

Jiri

Lukla

Kanchenjunga

Kathmandu

Bhaktapur

Those

SOLU KHUMBU

Bharatpur

Patan

Chitwan

KATHMANDU

Dhulikhel

Tadi

VALLEY

Saileri

Taplejung

Tiger Tops

Hetauda

Namobuddha

Sun Kosi River

Bhajpur

Terhathum

Darjeeling

Birganj

Simra

Arun River

Dhankuta

Ilam

Raxaul

A

Janakpur

Kosi River

Dharan

Kakarbitta

Jaya Nagar

Biratnagar

Jagbeni

Above the Terai rise the Siwalik foothills and beyond them the higher, more barren Mahabharat range. The bulk of the population of Nepal is found in the fertile intermontane valleys, such as the Kathmandu Valley and the Pokhara Valley, north of the Mahabharat range and at altitudes between 1000 and 2000 m. North again rises the sweep of the Himalayan range forming a barrier between Tibet and Nepal. In general the border runs along the peaks of the range, Mt Everest straddles the border, but in western Nepal at the country's widest point a portion of the high arid Tibetan plateau forms the legendary Mustang province. The Terai also disappears at a point where the Indian border comes right up to the Siwalik foothills.

Tamang Girl

The population of Nepal is about 12 million and that of Kathmandu, the main city, about 300,000. Like the geography the population of the country is extremely diverse. Some tribes, such as the Sherpas living in the eastern Everest region, have won fame as mountaineers while others, like the Gurungs, Magars and Chetris in the west and the Rais and Limbus in the east, have made their mark as Gurkha soldiers. The original inhabitants of the Kathmandu Valley, the Newars, have made significant contributions in the development of art and architecture. Nepalese living in the Terai have close ethnic and linguistic ties with people across the border in the Bihar and Uttar Pradesh states of India.

Nepal's main exports are rice and jute which are grown in the Terai. Tourism is now superseding the Gurkha earnings as Nepal's chief foreign currency earner. Mineral wealth in Nepal appears to be limited and inaccessible, a result of the country's geological newness. Nepal has vast potential for the development of hydroelectric power.

Development in Nepal is concentrated on improvements in communications, agriculture and education. The road building programme is continuing to link previously isolated parts of the country. In agriculture the green revolution has had a major impact on Nepal, particularly in the fertile but heavily populated Kathmandu Valley which is now able to feed itself. Nevertheless Nepal's steep population growth will continue to put pressure on agricultural potential.. Birth control programmes are a major part of the educational development which it is hoped will reduce the illiteracy rate from its current levels of over 70% amongst males and over 90% amongst females.

Life expectancy at birth was only 40 years in Nepal in 1970. Much remains to be done to increase the number of hospitals and doctors as there is only one doctor for each 96,000 people. As most of the doctors are living in Kathmandu, this disparity is even more extreme in the remote areas of the country.

## CULTURE AND CUSTOMS

Nepal is the meeting place of two great religions, Hinduism and Buddhism; two races, caucasian and mongoloid; and two civilizations, Indic and Sinic. The population has a variety of ethnic groups each with distinct cultural identity.

Polygamy was, and still is, practised in many areas of the country although legislation has banned it in the last decade. In the northern hill areas polyandry, the practise of a wife having more than one husband was also practised. Ethnic groups such as the Brahmins and Chetris are prohibited from drinking alcohol and sometimes follow vegetarian restraints. Widow remarriage and cousin marriages are not socially acceptable in some groups and amongst Brahmin families a man first meets his wife on the day he gets married. On the other hand the Gurung group have an institution called *Rodighar* intended to bring people together before they contemplate marriage. The Sherpas have a remarkably free and easy moral code.

When going inside Nepali homes it is polite to remove your shoes. Westerners should not try to enter Hindu temples and never touch the deity although they are quite free to watch from outside. Public displays of affection are not good manners nor should one swim naked in lakes or rivers. As in many parts of Asia the sight of men and boys walking hand in hand is quite normal and does not have the same meaning it does in the west. Many young Nepalese children have started coming to trekkers and asking for money, this is one of the bad effects of tourism and should not be encouraged. The speed and intensity of change in Nepal in the past two decades has been surprising and it will be a great shame if this process of westernisation has too great an effect on Nepal's unique culture.

> To anyone deeply interested in Tibetan Buddhism it is a Tibetan custom to visit the Rimpoche (reincarnate lama) of the nearby monastery. Generally the purpose is to receive his blessings and consult him concerning important matters, often to ask questions concerning dharma and sometimes only to take an offering to the monastery. A Khata gift scarf, available at any Tibetan shop for about Rs 1.50, is always taken, usually with a donation of butter or tea or perhaps money wrapped inside the scarf. This is presented to the Rimpoche held loosely between both hands.
>
> *Philip Wolcott, USA*

## RELIGION

Hinduism and Buddhism are the two important religions in Nepal. The majority of the population are Hindus but the religions are closely intertwined and many Nepalese profess both religions at the same time. Buddhists are mainly found along the northern border area and in the eastern part of the country. Hindus are most numerous in the south and west. There are a small number, about 3% of the population, of Moslems mainly concentrated along the border with India although there are also scattered Moslem villages.

## HINDU DEITIES

The Hindu religion has a large and confusing number of Gods and their attendant consorts and animals. Understanding is simplified if you bear in mind that each represents some God like attribute. The three main Gods are Brahma the creator, Vishnu the preserver and Shiva the destroyer and regenerator. Brahma, whose consort is Saraswati, is not as revered in Nepal as he is in India. Each of the Gods has a number of incarnations and there are several incarnations which are unique to Nepal.

**Vishnu** Also known as Narayan, Vishnu can be identified by his four arms holding a *sankha* (sea shell), *chakra* (round weapon), gada (stick like weapon) and *padma* (lotus flower). Vishnu's animal is the mythical man-bird known as the Garuda; a Garuda will often be found close by a temple to Vishnu.

The most important temple of Vishnu in the valley is Changunarayan but there is also a very good image of the "sleeping" Vishnu at Budhanilkantha. Vishnu has ten incarnations one of which is Krishna, who is often blue — there is a particularly well known Krishna Temple in the Durbar Square of Patan. Narsimha, the man-lion is another incarnation of Vishnu, see the beautiful image inside the old Royal Palace. Some Hindus consider Buddha to be one of the ten incarnations of Vishnu. Vishnu's wife, Laxmi, is the Goddess of Wealth according to Hindu mythology.

**Shiva** Pashupatinath, which is another name for the God, is the best known temple to Shiva in the valley. Shiva is often represented by the *lingam,* a phallic symbol of his creative side. Shiva's animal is the bull, Nandi, and there is a giant sized Nandi in front of Pashupatinath. The image of Pashupatinath itself contains five heads, this is not common in other temples of Shiva. The weapon of Shiva is the *trisul* or trident. According to Hindu mythology Shiva is supposed to live in the Himalayas, smoke a lot of hashish and wear a garland of snakes. Bhairab is a representation of the terrible form of Shiva and there are numerous images of Bhairab in the valley.

**Parvati** Parvati is the consort of Shiva and like her God she has a peaceful and a fearful side to her activities. She is shown in her terrible form holding a variety of weapons and her animal is the lion. Dasain, celebrated in her honour, is characterised by the sacrifice of hundreds of animals. Daxinkali is the best known of her temples.

**Hanuman** The monkey god Hanuman is the legendary figure from the epic Ramayana who helped rescue Rama's wife Sita from the clutches of the demon Rawana. Rama is yet another of the incarnations of Vishnu and Hanuman was his faithful servant. An image of Hanuman guards the Hanuman Dhoka, entrance to the old Royal Palace of Kathmandu.

**Ganesh** Easily recognised by his elephant head, Ganesh, the God of Learning, has many temples in Nepal. The animal of Ganesh, which he rides as his "vehicle", is the mouse! In the course of general worship Ganesh is the first of the deities to be worshipped and the Maru Ganesh temple near Durbar Square in Kathmandu is visited by a large number of devotees from dawn to late at night.

Shiva, Ganesh's father, is said to have returned to his wife Parvati after a journey lasting fourteen years. Arriving home at night he found Parvati asleep with a young boy beside her. Suspecting her of infidelity he immediately lopped off the boy's head and then discovered it was his own son. Shiva was very sad and said he would bring his son back to life if the first living thing seen in the morning was brought to him. The first living thing turned out to be an elephant and Shiva took its head and joined it to the trunk of his son who became Ganesh.

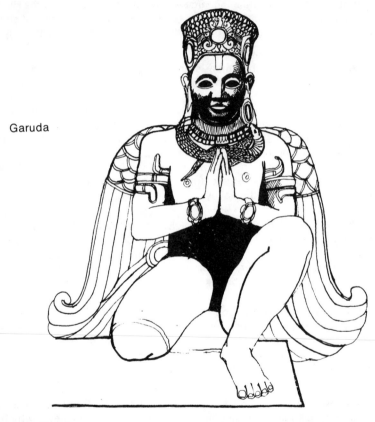

Garuda

**Garuda** The Garuda is well known for its aerial abilities and its intense hatred of snakes — Garuda devours snakes at the door of almost all the temples of Kathmandu. You will see a Garuda in front of temples of Vishnu. Indonesia has named its national airline Garuda after this same famous man-bird but the Indonesian Garuda is less man and more bird than the Nepalese variety.

## FESTIVALS IN NEPAL

Few people in the world can celebrate as many festivals as the Newars of Kathmandu Valley. Hardly a month passes without a major festival or feast but the three months from August to October is a real festival season and you're bound to see some picturesque festival if you visit Nepal during that time. Major festivals include:

### August

**Gai Jatra or Cow Festival:** Hundreds of garlanded and costumed people walk in a long procession accompanied by cows and crowds of happy people. If there has been a death in the family it is expected that a group consisting of two people, usually a boy and a person dressed as a *sadhu* (saint), and a cow, will be sent to participate in the day-long festival. This curious practise originated from the belief that people who happen to be holding a cow's tail at the moment of death have precedence at the hall of justice!

**Krishnasthami:** The best place to watch the celebrations of Krishna's birthday is at the Krishna temple in Patan. Sacred devotional music is played all night if you can manage to stay awake; go in the evening.

**Teej:** This is a special festival for women and all married women are supposed to fast all day and bathe in the holy waters of the rivers. The entrance to Pashupatinath is a good place to watch as crowds of women, dressed in brightly coloured saris with red marks on their foreheads, come down to the river. It is believed that their married life will be long and happy and they will not lose their husbands if they celebrate this festival. Red is a symbol of joy and happiness in Nepal and the colour used for marriage ceremonies. Married women are expected to wear a lot of red but widows are forbidden to do so; white is the colour of mourning in Nepal.

> Thousands of women dressed in red saris flock to the temple of Pashupatinath on fasting day to do their obeisance to Shiva and his consort Parvati. One or two days later there is the ritual of washing in the holy waters of the Bagmati River in which everyone washes everything 360 times. One can go, unobtrusively, to the more sacred spots on the river bank and witness the marvellous crowds of women singing and joyously cleansing their bodies and souls.
>
> *Meg Levine, USA*

### September

**Indrajatra:** The Indra festival, in honour of the ancient Aryan God Indra,

God of Rain, marks the end of the monsoon and the beginning of the best season of the year, which lasts for two months. The living goddess, Kumari, is taken in procession through the streets of Kathmandu and the king receives blessings from her. The image of White Bhairab, behind the Black Bhairab in Kathmandu's Durbar Square, is unveiled for three days each year during this festival. Traditional Newar folk dances are performed in the streets around the Durbar Square, Basantapur Square and the Indrachok area. On this same day, in 1768, King Prithvi Narayan Shah conquered Kathmandu and took the major step in the process of unifying Nepal. The festival continues for four days.

## October
**Bada Dasain:** This is the biggest festival in Nepal and lasts 15 days in all although the main festivities are concentrated in nine days during which all schools and government offices are closed. On the seventh day called "Fulpati", you can see around noon or early afternoon, a procession of government officials in national dress preceded by a band from the old Royal Palace in Durbar Square. On the ninth day, thousands of goats and buffaloes are sacrificed around noon in the courtyard called "Kot" behind Durbar Square and a stream of blood flows. Similar sacrifices are made in the temples of goddesses throughout the country and on this day, every household in Nepal eats meat. The tenth day, Bijaya Dashami is the highlight of the festival and all Hindus and many Buddhists go to their relatives and elders in order to receive a "tika", which is rice immersed in a red liquid, placed on their forehead. On the streets of Kathmandu on this day you will hardly see a person who does not wear this red mark. In late afternoon, if you walk two blocks from Durbar Square to the temple of Naradevi, you can see the Festival of the Sword (Khadga Jatra). This day is supposed to represent the victory of good over evil, according to legend the Goddess Durga killed a demon on this day.

The final day of the festival, a full moon day, is marked by much gambling in some Nepalese households. Dasain is not only the biggest festival but a happy one because the weather is perfect, and the rice is ready to be harvested. It is a pleasant time for walking in the hills which makes the visits to relatives doubly enjoyable. In the villages large swings will be set up for the children to play on.

## November
**Tihar:** The third and fifth days are the most important of this five-day festival. In western India it is the biggest Hindu festival and in Nepal it is second only to Dasain. On the first day crows, the messengers of death, are honoured and fed. The second day is in honour of dogs, the guardians of the dead and the mount of Bh'airab. The third day is set aside for cows

as the incarnation of Laxmi. This day is called Deepavali, the festival of lights, and all the households of Kathmandu are illuminated by lamps to the Goddess of Wealth. This festival always falls on a new moon so the effect is particularly delightful. It is said that the Goddess Laxmi will shun any household not illuminated on this day, which is also an occasion for gambling.

The new year for the Newars of the valley also starts from this day. The Nepalese national new year starts on 13 April and 1976 in western terms is 2033 in Nepalese. The Newari calendar equates 1976 to 1096. The Tibetans living in Nepal also have their own calendar.

The fifth day of the festival is Bhai Tika and is meant especially for brothers and sisters who are supposed to get together on this day. There is a small ceremony and they mark each others foreheads with *tikas*. The sister also puts oil on her brother's forehead and offers sweets and fruits, in return he pays her small sums of money, say Rs 5 or 10. On this day the bazaars of Kathmandu are full of sweets and fresh and dry fruits.

**Ekadashi:**    On the eleventh day after the new moon Vishnu is supposed to wake up after having slept for four months. There will be many pilgrims at Pashupatinath but the best place to view this festival is at the temple of Changunarayan or at the temple of the sleeping Vishnu at Budhanilkantha. The activities at Budhanilkantha are equally interesting on the next day when a long line of devotees queue to touch the feet of the deity.

## December

**Bala Chaturdashi:** People come from all over the valley and beyond to the temple of Pashupatinath to take part in a ceremony which consists of scattering seeds of different kinds in memory of their dead relatives. The evening is the best time to observe the ceremony as you will see many pilgrims performing religious rites and singing and dancing.

## February

**Tibetan New Year:** There are religious celebrations in Bodnath Stupa around noontime and the Buddhist monks give blessings. This festival is essentially a family affair when friends and members of the family get together.

**Maha Shivaratri:** The birthday of Lord Shiva usually falls in the cold month of February but many pilgrims come from the warm weather of the terai or the north Indian plains to worship at the temple of Pashupatinath in a colourful yet deeply serene ceremony.

> During the festival of Sivaratri, the most impressive feature was the mass of colour and simple dignity of the pilgrims as they performed the ritual bathing in the holy river. Some Sadhus covered with ashes lay on a bed of thorns and also impaled their tongues with thorns.
>
> *John Hayward, England*

## March

**Holi or Fagu:** This festival of rejoicing occurs in the springtime on the day of the full moon in the Nepalese month of Falgun when a pillar is installed in Basantapur Square in front of the old Royal Palace. The festival used to last for eight days and was marked by throwing coloured water and red powder on acquaintances and even people passing by on the street. The festival now takes place only on the day of the full moon but visitors should watch out for the coloured water! If you happen to be on the Helambu trek the village of Tarkeghyang has a colourful festival celebrated with dancing and singing until the late hours. The Sherpas in the mountains do without the water throwing.

## April

**Chaitra Dasain:** Also called small Dasain in contrast to October's big Dasain, this festival is similar in many respects and many goats and buffalos will be sacrificed to the Goddess Durga at the Kot Square. An image of the Goddess is pulled on a chariot through the streets.

**Bisket Festival:**  A wooden pillar is erected in the evening on the first day of this Bhaktapur festival. On the second day, which is also the first day of the year by the Nepalese calendar, a chariot is pulled from the pillar to the temple of Bhairabnath in the same square as the five-storey Nyatapola pagoda. The chariot is very old and looks on the point of collapse — as it is pulled every part shakes violently and it makes a tremendous spectacle. The pillar is shaken violently in the evening and then lowered with great rejoicing. The chariots of Ganesh and the Goddesses Mahakali and Mahalaxmi are carried on the shoulders of the devotees.

## May

**Birthday of Buddha:** Since Nepal is the birthplace of Buddha and there are still many Buddhists amongst the Nepalese this festival is celebrated with especial pomp. Swayambhunath and Bodhnath are particularly popular centres and pilgrims will gather at Swayambhunath from early in the morning.

**Rato Machhendranath:**    The festival of Red Machhendranath takes place in Patan over a period of two months and is one of the most complex festivals. During the celebrations a chariot bearing the image of Machhendranath, revered by Hindus and Buddhists, moves in a series of daily stages through the streets of Patan.

### July

**Naga Panchami:** Images of the serpent Naga are stuck over the doors of houses during the festival of snakes. Since snakes are believed to have power over the monsoon rainfall it is important that they are propitiated — their image also keeps evil from entering the home.

**Janai Purnima:**    All high caste Hindus wear a sacred thread over their left shoulder and tied under their right armpit. On this day each year the sacred thread is replaced after a day-long fast. Kumbheswara temple in Patan and the holy lake of Gosainkunda are important places for this festival.

> Two times a month on the eleventh day after the full moon and the new moon, a concert of classical Indian music is given in the Narayan Temple very near the new Royal Palace. The best Nepalese musicians, especially tabla and sitar, and several singers of all ages will sing in the evening.
>
> *Nadine Beautheac, France*

**Marriage Ceremony:**    Marriage ceremonies in Nepal are supposed to take place only in five months of the year — mid-January to mid-March, mid-April to mid-June and mid-November to mid-December. Astrologers select auspicious dates within these periods on the basis of the positions of the stars. It is quite common to see several marriage processions on the same particularly auspicious occasion. The marriage ritual differs in the various communities but almost always has a procession preceded by a band. The bridegroom spends a night at the bride's house where a big religious ceremony is held during which the bride and groom walk around a fire on a platform so that the fire "witnesses" their marriage.

### FESTIVAL CALENDAR

Almost all of the festivals in Nepal are celebrated according to the lunar calendar so it is difficult to tell in advance the exact dates when they will take place. The festival calendar, made after consulting the lunar calendar, covers major festivals for 1978, 1979 and 1980.

| Name of Festival | Place |
|---|---|
| Bisketjatra — Festival of Bisket | Bhaktapur |
| Buddha Jayanti — Birthday of Buddha | Swayambhu |
| Gaijatra — Cow Festival | Kathmandu |
| Krishnasthami — Birthday of Krishna | Patan |
| Teej — Festival of Women | Pashupatinath |
| drajatra — Indra Festival | Kathmandu |
| de Dasain — Big Dasain | All over Nepal |
| Navami | Kathmandu |
| Bijaya Dashami | All over Nepal |
| — Festival of Light | All over Nepal |
| Bhai Tika | All over Nepal |
| Harit ani Ekadashi — Big Ekadashi | Budhanilkantha & Changunarayan |
| Bala Cha Iashi | Pashupatinath |
| Maha Shiv i — Birthday of Shiva | Pashupatinath |
| Holi — Festi Colour | All over Nepal Tarke in Helambu |
| Ghodejatra — Fes of Horse Racing | Kathmandu |
| Chaitra Dasain — Sr Dasain | All over Nepal — Old Palace, Kat |
| Tibetan New Year | Bodhnath |
| Mani Rimdu | Solu Khumbu |

The following table shows the dates when Ekadashi is supposed to fall — the eleventh day after each full and new moon. On these days there is classical music played in the Narayan Temple near the new Royal Palace in Kathmandu and various events in the evening at the temple of Pashupatinath.

| | Jan | Feb | Mar | Apr | May |
|---|---|---|---|---|---|
| 1978 | 5, 19 | 4, 18 | 5, 20 | 3, 19 | 3, 18 |
| 1979 | 9, 24 | 7, 23 | 9, 24 | 8, 23 | 8, 22 |

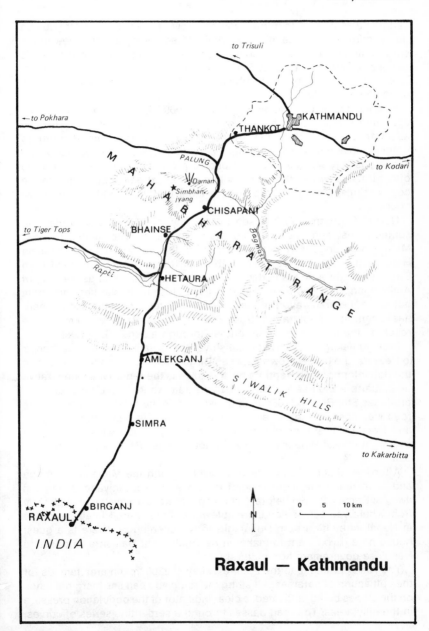

**Raxaul — Kathmandu**

can find a spare seat in a truck you can travel for Rs 15 to 20. Or you can go by more comfortable mini-bus for Rs 40 and enjoy a better view of the surroundings. Several bus companies operate this route, some of the better ones are Das, Yatayat Sansthan and Pradhan Transport. Try to get a seat within the bus wheelbase, seats right at the back give an uncomfortable ride.

Birganj has a population of about 30,000. A sugar factory and an agricultural implements factory have been constructed here with Russian assistance. The Tribhuvan Rajpath runs 200 km from Birganj to Kathmandu and reaches a maximum altitude of over 2500 m. Although the scenery is very spectacular most people prefer not to make this trip too often, it takes over eight hours by bus and is extremely tiring due to the constant ups, downs and arounds. In a car the time could be cut to five hours.

North of Birganj you can see the heavily forested Siwalik Hills, The southernmost and youngest mountains in Nepal. The almost treeless Mahabharat range is visible beyond and if the weather is clear the main Himalayan range can be seen further still to the north. The road from Birganj runs through the flatlands known as the *Terai* as far as the town of Amlekhganj. The people in this area have close linguistic ties with India but since the eradication of malaria in the *Terai* during the sixties there has been much migration from the hill country. Eleven km before reaching the foothills the road passes through a dense Sal forest.

From Amlekhganj the road climbs over the Siwalik hills then descends to Hetaura, the biggest town between Birganj and Kathmandu. Situated in the rich intermontane Rapti Valley this town is the regional administrative headquarters and has a small industrial estate where Nepal's first brewery produces Star Beer with German assistance. In the 1920s, long before the road was constructed, an aerial ropeway was built between Kathmandu and Hetaura. It still carries goods to this day. If you wish to make an overnight stay at Hetaura the *Hotel Rapti* charges Rs 12 for a single with bath.

After the village of Bhainse you travel through the Mahabharat range and soon reach the highest point known as Sim Bhanjyang. A few km away at Daman, 80 km before Kathmandu, there is a view tower at 2300 m from where you can see an incredible view of the entire Himalayan range in Nepal, stretching from Dhaulagiri to Kanchenjunga. There is a guest house here if you want to make an overnight halt. Daman also boasts a Nepalese government horticultural farm.

The road continues to the Palung Valley at 2300 m, an area famous for the cultivation of potatoes. All along the route you can see marginal lands on the slopes being cultivated, a clear indicator of the population pressure in the hilly areas. The road passes through a serpentine series of curves, known as *seven turns* in Nepal, before descending to the tropical valley of Dhunibesi at 750 m. The valley is an important producer of guavas, mangoes and bananas and from the town of Naubise in this valley the road to Pokhara branches off. A steep 700 m climb takes you over the final hill before descending to Thankot the first village in the Kathmandu valley and only a short drive from the city.

If you want to fly between Birganj and Kathmandu take the short bus ride to Simra where the airport is located. RNAC make two flights a day on this short ( less than half an hour) sector; cost is Rs 90.

## TO POKHARA FROM NAUTANWA

Only two trains travel to the Indian border town of Nautanwa each day, from there you must take a bus or share a taxi to Sunauli which is situated right on the border. Alternately you can take a bus from Gorakhpur directly to the border. After crossing the border a rickshaw to the town of Bhairawa will cost Rs 2. Since the buses to Pokhara only leave in the morning you will probably have to spend the night here. Singles at the *Pashupati Lodge* run Rs 10 to 15 a single or you can stay at the *Machhapuchhare.*

The road from Bhairawa to Lumbini, the birthplace of Buddha, is expected to be completed in early 1978. If you visit Bhairawa during the dry season it is worth making the effort to follow the 25 km trail to Lumbini. I met an American girl who walked to Lumbini in 6 hours and stayed there overnight, you could possibly hire a bicycle. There are two small rivers to cross on the way but even without bridges they are easily fordable in winter. The entire Lumbini region is expected to be developed with UN assistance in a few years time. In 249 BC, when he had been annointed for 20 years, King Devanam Priya Priyadarshin (Ashoka — Emperor of India) came to worship here at Buddha's birthplace and erected a giant pillar.

At 7, 9 and 11 express buses leave Bhairawa for Pokhara and charge Rs 25. It is better to backtrack to Sunauli on the border where the buses start to make certain of getting a good seat. From the town of Butwal a few km to the north buses leave almost every hour but take longer to reach Pokhara as they operate a local service. An express bus also runs from Bhairawa straight through Pokhara to Kathmandu which it reaches the same evening.

Like the road between Birganj and Kathmandu the road was constructed with Indian assistance and is about 200 km long. It is, however, a better road. The road crosses the Terai to Butwal then climbs over the Siwalik and Mahabharat ranges. Two hours out you reach the beautiful town of Tansen on a hillock at 1271 m, pleasantly cool if you have just left the hot Indian plains. Around the bus terminal you can have a meal at one of many good *bhattis,* hotels run by the local Thakalis. A five

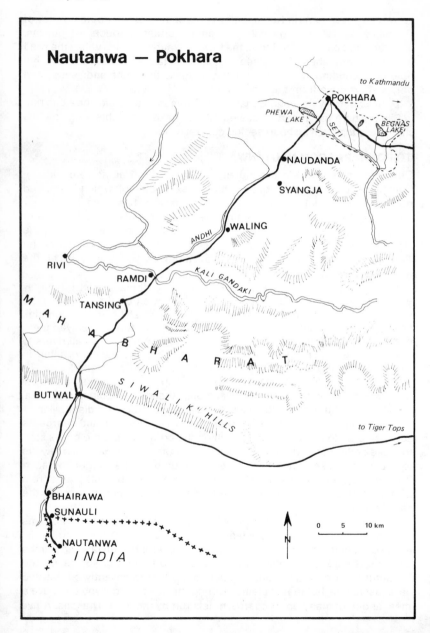

**Nautanwa — Pokhara**

minute walk along a steep slope will take you to *Janapriya Hotel* if you wish to stop for the night. If you do stop then make sure of climbing the hillock, known as Srinagar, to admire the Himalayan view stretching from Dhaulagiri to Manaslu. Tansen is a small town inhabited mainly by Newars. It used to be the most important town in west central Nepal and was the administrative headquarters for the area.

Continuing northwards the road passes through the small town of Arya Bhanjyange then descends steeply to the Kali Gandaki River, one of Nepal's largest, and crosses it at Ramdighat at 375 m.

A series of ascents takes you to Waling at 700 m, a town which has grown tremendously after the construction of the road. The road then passes through the towns of Syangja and Naudanda, the starting point for a trail to Kusma and Baglung. There is, incidentally, another Naudanda on the direct trail from Pokhara to the Annapurna sanctuary and Jomosom. The road finally enters the Pokhara Valley from the south.

It is also possible to fly between Bhairawa and Pokhara. RNAC have flights on Monday, Wednesday, Friday and Sunday — the cost is Rs 100. Bhairawa to Kathmandu via Pokhara will set you back Rs 250.

If you plan to trek in the Pokhara area it is preferable to enter Nepal from Raxaul as trekking permits are only obtainable in Kathmandu. Coming this way you would have to continue on to Kathmandu to get your permit.

## TO KATHMANDU FROM DARJEELING

You can also enter Nepal from Kakarbitta near the eastern border across the Mechi River which forms the boundary with India. A bus or jeep will take you to the border from the Indian town of Siliguri. Buses to Kathmandu from Kakarbitta cost Rs 67, student card holders get a 25% discount, and take at least two days including an overnight stop at the Terai town of Janakpur. Until you meet the Birganj to Kathmandu road this route runs through the Terai just a few km south of the Siwalik Hills. Dense forest and new settlements are visible north of the road and the bus also passes through Biratnagar a major industrial area and the centre of the jute industry. Later you will see the beautiful foothill town of Dharan and cross the barrages of the mighty Kosi River which causes much damage by flooding. The road as far as Janakpur was constructed under Indian assistance and from there to the intersection north of Birganj was constructed by the Russians. This route is often impossible in the monsoon as there are few bridges built yet. It is possible to fly from Bhadrapur, only a short bus ride from Kakarbitta, to Kathmandu on Mondays and Fridays for Rs 200. The flight departs at 9.45am and there is a Rs 10 domestic airport tax.

## OVERLAND TRAVEL

Many people pass through Nepal on their way east or west on the well-known Asian overland route. Travelling independently by bus or train, in their own vehicles — usually Land Rovers or VW Kombis, or on one of the many organised overland expeditions, thousands of people make this exciting journey each year.

Travelling west from Kathmandu the usual route is through New Delhi in India and across the border to Lahore in Pakistan. The route continues through Peshawar in the Pathan region of Pakistan then climbs over the historic Khyber Pass into Afghanistan. From the Afghan capital of Kabul the road runs south to Kandahar then turns north again to Herat before crossing the border to Mashed in Iran. Continuing west you travel to the capital Tehran and on to Tabriz but most travellers detour south for a visit to the beautiful city of Isfahan and the ancient ruins of Persepolis. After entering Turkey there is a choice of routes but most people pass through Erzurum and the capital Ankara before finally leaving Asia at the Bosphorus crossing in Turkey.

Travelling east from Nepal most travellers fly to Bangkok, often with a week's stop-off in Burma, then travel down through Thailand and Malaysia to Singapore. Frequent flights and a weekly ship link Singapore with Jakarta the capital of Indonesia. There are several routes across Java through Yogyakarta and on to the magical island of Bali. More adventurous travellers can "island hop" south from Bali to Australia or cross over to Sumatra from Penang in Malaysia and travel the length of that wild Indonesian island before reaching Jakarta. Details of travel in both directions from Nepal can be found in *Across Asia on the Cheap* and *South-East Asia on a Shoestring* both published by Lonely Planet Publications.

A number of companies operate expeditions from Kathmandu to London and vice versa over a variety of routes and at a wide range of costs. Average time from Kathmandu to London is 90 days but there are shorter and longer trips. A few of the organisers are:

*Penn Overland*
122 Knightsbridge Rd    177 Collins St    34th Floor
London SW1    Melbourne    Australia Square
England    Australia    Sydney, Australia

*Sundowners*
8 Hogarth Place    317 Little Collins St    75 King St
London SW5    41 Block Place    Sydney
England    Melbourne, Australia    Australia

*Trail Finders*
| | | |
|---|---|---|
| 46-48 Earls Court Rd | 3 Manchester Lane | 15 Hunter St |
| London W8 | Melbourne | Sydney |
| England | Australia | Australia |

*Treasure Tours*
| | | |
|---|---|---|
| 40-42 Willis St | 344 Queens St | As Trail Finder for |
| Wellington | Auckland | Sydney & Melbourne |
| New Zealand | New Zealand | |

Other companies operating overland include *Capricorn Overland, Intertrek, Exodus, Encounter Overland, Asian Greyhound* and *Hughes Overland*. Many of the overland companies will have offices, representatives or meeting points in Kathmandu.

## ENTERING NEPAL BY AIR

Kathmandu is off line for all the international airlines. Most air travellers from Europe will fly up from Delhi by Royal Nepal Airlines or Indian Airlines. Travellers from North America or Australasia generally enter from Bangkok by Thai International, Burma Airways Corporation or Royal Nepal Airlines. It is also possible to fly to Kathmandu from Rangoon in Burma, Dacca in Bangladesh or Calcutta, Varanasi and Patna in India.

Airfares in early 1978 were:

| | | |
|---|---|---|
| Bangkok | — Kathmandu | $US243.00 |
| Delhi | — Kathmandu | $US 87.60 |
| Calcutta | — Kathmandu | $US 58.20 |
| Patna | — Kathmandu | $US 23.80 |
| Varanasi | — Kathmandu | $US 42.90 |
| Colombo | — Kathmandu | $US215.00 |
| Dacca | — Kathmandu | $US 61.80 |

Flying from Bangkok it is possible to include at no extra cost, a seven day stopover in Burma. Visas for Burma can be obtained in Bangkok or Kathmandu. International Student Card holders under 26 years of age are allowed a 25% reduction on external and internal flights of Royal Nepal Airlines and Indian Airlines.

Travelling between Kathmandu and Delhi the budget conscious traveller can more than halve his costs by flying to Patna and then continuing by train to Delhi in less than 24 hours. Total cost by this method will be less than $US30. Curiously the cost of a Kathmandu-Patna and a Patna-Delhi ticket is also less than a direct Kathmandu-Delhi flight. By travelling this way, a saving of $US20 can be made. It is possible to make Patna-Delhi reservation for the same day's flight from Kathmandu.

The flight into Nepal will give you a superb view of the mountains in clear weather — if you choose the correct side of the aircraft. Flying from the east — Bangkok, Rangoon or Calcutta — try to be on the right side of the aircraft. If you are flying from the west — New Delhi or Varanasi — then try to be on the left side of the aircraft. Kathmandu's international airport is named Tribhuvan Airport after the late king but used to rejoice in the name Gaucher, cow pasture, field!

## ENTRY AND EXIT

Nepali customs are fairly lax on entry but quite systematic on departure to ensure visitors do not export antique works of art or marijuana. The usual, rarely enforced, regulations apply to how much of what you're allowed to bring in to the country. The only requirement it might be advisable to worry about is the per person limit of twelve rolls of film. If you will be considerably over these limits it may be wise to check with the Nepalese embassy before departure.

On departure there is a Rs 40 airport tax, domestic flights are also subject to a Rs 10 airport tax. The airport has a duty free shop selling the usual range of cigarettes and liquor which must be paid for in US dollars. The experienced shoestring traveller will no doubt be familiar with the considerably greater value of these items in other Asian countries. A carton of 555 cigarettes and bottle of Johnny Walker Red Label is a very advisable investment if Burma is your next stop.

If you are departing by land and will be travelling by Indian rail *Gurung Transport Company*, next to the Unity Restaurant, can reserve seats and sleepers from Raxaul or Patna via their agents there. This will avoid the possibility of delay on the often heavily booked Indian trains. Approximate costs and times for rail travel, 2nd to 1st class, between major Indian cities and the rail heads for Nepal are:

**for Kathmandu**
| | | |
|---|---|---|
| Calcutta-Raxaul | 23 hours | Rs 27 to Rs 90 |

**for Pokhara**
| | | |
|---|---|---|
| New Delhi-Agra | 3 hours | |
| Agra-Varanasi | 13 hours | Rs 38 to Rs 132 |
| Varanasi-Nautawa | 11 hours | |

cars. Arjun, the manager, speaks Japanese and most of the clientele of the hotel are either German or Japanese. *Serenity Inn* (tel 14306) in the same area charges Rs 15 bathless singles.

### Rock Bottom Hotels

The wide range of new hotels and lodges in this category offer excellent opportunities for good but inexpensive accommodation for the low budget traveller. So many have opened recently that it is becoming increasingly difficult for their clientele of students, young travellers and freaks to make a choice. The intense competition has led to the provision of some minimum facilities like hot showers.

Most of the lodges in this category can be found in the Freak Street or Pig Alley area. Some budget travellers prefer not to stay around Freak Street and there are a few places scattered around other parts of Kathmandu.

**Freak Street:** In the heart of Freak Street is the *Oriental Lodge* (tel 12168) one of the best places in this category. A single room here costs Rs 8 and a hot shower Rs 1. Right next to the Oriental is the *Century Lodge*, rather quieter as it is in the interior, away from the main street. The prices are similar and there is a library with many books in English available to residents. Suman Shrestha, the amiable manager, is a good source of information on interesting places to see in the valley. Across the street is the *Monumental Lodge* (tel 13065) where a single costs Rs 8 and hot showers are thrown in for free. The *Annapurna Lodge* is in the same street and charges from Rs 5 to 8 for a single room. The *Everest Lodge* in Freak Street charges Rs 10 for a single and Rs 12 for a double.

**Pig Alley:** Pig Alley, as Maru Tole has been nicknamed by westerners, is the street containing all the pie shops. It may not look very clean but it does have two good lodges which are popular with many budget travellers. The *Delight Lodge* (tel 15267) charges Rs 10 to 12 for a single or Rs 5 for a bed in the dormitory. The *Guardian Lodge* costs Rs 7 for a single.

**Elsewhere:** A block from New Road and opposite the Mt Makalu Hotel is *City Lodge* where a single costs Rs 8 and a double Rs 15. T K Sakya, who runs this popular lodge, offers advice on trekking and free storage of luggage while you're away on trek. Also very good is the *Kathmandu Lodge* (tel 13868), in the Durbar Square area where a single costs Rs 15 and a double Rs 25. It is popular even with those who are not travelling on a budget. Recommended. Two blocks from Durbar Square and well away from any other lodge is the *Travellers Lodge* where singles cost Rs 8 to 16. Rooms on the top floor are sunny in winter and have good views of

Kathmandu City. *Hotel Swiss Cottage* (tel 14167) is in Chetrapati and has singles at Rs 20.

The *Blue Angel Hotel* (tel 14269) is near the Post Office, just a block from the tower its large and sunny rooms have a good view of the area and attract many travellers who have tried other lodges first. A single costs Rs 15. Recommended. In the same area, the *Lagan Lodge* is also popular.

If you've come to Kathmandu by car and want cheap accommodation plus car parking space the *Happy Lodge* is situated in quiet surroundings across the river in Tahachal — on the road to Swayambhu. *Withies Hotel* (tel 13839) is situated at Tekh just as you enter Kathmandu by road from Pokhara or the Indian border, it also offers car parking space.

Some of the lodges at the bottom of the rock bottom range are situated in localities which could hardly be called "clean" as it is understood in the west. On the other hand if you want to live in more indigenious, even medieval, surroundings you may well like them. As far as I know, the lodges are quite clean and well cared for and, of course, very inexpensive. A single room can cost as little as Rs 4 although living there is certain to brand you a hippy.

Near the river Bishnumati, three blocks from Durbar Square, is *Hotch Potch Lodge*. The *Match Box* and *New Match Box Lodges* are in the same Pig Alley area.

At Jawlakhel, near the zoo and about fifteen minutes walk from the Patan bus stop is the *Youth Hostel* (tel 21003). If you want to live inexpensively and don't mind being some distance from Kathmandu a dormitory bed costs just Rs 5 or a double room Rs 15.

If you are planning a longer stay it is possible to rent a private home for as little as Rs 50 a month. Main areas are Swayambhu, Bodhnath or in Freak Street although you can also find long term accommodation in other areas. If you wish to rent a room or apartment contact Major Rana (tel 11542) or find him at his home in Lagen, one block from Freak Street, between 7 and 8am. He does not charge any commission to the lessee. A casual wander around Swayambhunath will usually turn some place up — kids will soon find you. There are various noticeboards which may have information on places to rent — the Unity Restaurant, Aunt Janes, Kathmandu Guest House, Peace Corps Office are just a few. It's often better to take over a place from a departing traveller since finding second hand furniture may be difficult. Since fridges are virtually unavailable and incredibly expensive, as is electricity, it is wise to ensure that a market is reasonably close to hand for fresh food.

## WHERE TO EAT

Kathmandu's restaurants offer an amazing variety of foods. Most overland travellers find the food in Kathmandu to be better and more delicious than anywhere east of Istanbul. Where else in the middle of nowhere could you get sheesh kebab (Afghan), wienerschnitzel (German or Austrian), bortsch (Russian), tandoori chicken (northern Indian), masala dosa (southern Indian), kothe (Tibetan), chow mien (Chinese), hamburgers, hot dogs, brownies and banana splits (American), spaghetti (Italian), chicken a la Provencal and chateaubriand (French), enchiladas (Mexican), sukiyaki (Japanese) and even dal bhat tarkari (Nepali)? Where else but Kathmandu?

Not only that but Kathmandu's unique pie shops specialise in making pies and cakes whose quality approaches those available in the west. This is all very surprising to a Kathmanduite who can remember when, in 1955, there was only one restaurant in all of Kathmandu! All this is indicative of the great changes that have taken place in Nepal since it ended its long isolation and flung its doors open to the world. The Tibetan refugees who entered Nepal during this period have been a strong factor in the development of Nepal as the mini-gastronomic paradise of south Asia; many of the Chinese and Tibetan restaurants are run by Tibetans. There are few places in the east where so many different dishes from so many countries can be found in so small a city.

## Quality Restaurants

Expensive but excellent describes the *Yak and Yeti Chimney Room* which was originally started by Boris; born in Russia he formerly ran the Royal Hotel — the only high class hotel for westerners in Nepal during the fifties. Undoubtedly one of the best restaurants in Nepal it is in an old Rana palace whose elaborately decorated hall has been converted into a dining room. Around the large open fire on a cold night the *Yak and Yeti* has plenty of atmosphere.

Situated in Lal Durbar, about three minutes walk from the Hotel de L'Annapurna it is often very crowded. Most of the *Yak and Yeti's* clientele consists of well-off tourists, diplomats and a few affluent Nepalese but some budget minded tourists do venture in to sample the delights of Nepal's unique restaurant. If you do wish to eat here without too great expenditure then try the Ukranian bortsch which is always delicious and only costs Rs 20. Other popular dishes include stroganoff at Rs 60, and a fish dish called bekti.

The *Himalchuli Room* of the Soaltee Oberoi Hotel serves some of the best food in Kathmandu. Among the more popular dishes are a typically Nepalese soup *Alu Tama*, for Rs 11, sliced chicken with bamboo shoots for Rs 36 and a tandoori-chicken-type Nepali dish called *Sekuwa* for Rs 34. A variety of Indian, Chinese, continental and Nepalese dishes are featured in the *Soaltee Oberoi's* excellent Rs 75 buffet lunch. Soup and dessert are included with the main dishes and there is no extra charge if you come back for seconds.

The Japanese restaurant *Kushi Fuji* is above the offices of Tiger Tops, in the same street as the Hotel de l'Annapurna. You can either take your shoes off and sit in traditional Japanese style or sit up at a table. Lunch here is excellent value, tempura or pork cutlet, soup, a bowl of rice and coffee only costs Rs 20. Dinner is rather more expensive, sukiyaki chicken costs Rs 30, although the food will be cooked right in front of you.

Every evening at seven the *Everest Cultural Society* at Lal Durbar arranges Nepalese folk dances. A typical Nepalese dinner, as eaten by a well-to-do Nepali at home, is served after the show for Rs 35. The meal includes rice, dal and not too spicy curry, vegetables, chutney, dessert (a pudding or a Nepalese dessert called Sikarni) and can be washed down with *raksi*. This is one of the best places to try authentic Nepalese food, particularly if you must be careful about your eating.

All the restaurants in this category serve well-prepared food and always boil their water — you will be very unlikely to become ill from a visit to one of these restaurants. In winter these places are heated, a luxury many of Kathmandu's hotels and restaurants do not offer.

## Moderately Priced Restaurants

Situated on the ground floor of the Crystal Hotel, the *Other Room* offers excellent western and Indian food and a pleasantly genteel atmosphere in the heart of Kathmandu. Favourite dishes include the chateaubriand (Rs 30 for two people), tandoori chicken (Rs 14), Kabuli nan, keema and pillao. Highly recommended as good value for money.

The *Indira Restaurant* on the first floor on New Road, is one of the older restaurants in Kathmandu and serves good Indian food. The elite of Nepalese society come here for a cup of tea and a snack while relaxing and talking, often quite crowded. This is one of the few places in Kathmandu visited by a large number of westerners in addition to many Nepalese.

The *Annapurna Coffee Shop* is located in the same compound as the Hotel de l'Annapurna and serves excellent coffee, pastries and, for Rs 13, very special chiliburgers. The coffee shop's walls are decorated with scenes showing Nepalese dancers and it is kept pleasantly warm in winter. Around noon it is often crowded with westerners and affluent Nepalese. On the same street as the Hotel de l'Annapurna is the *Rara Restaurant* where moderately expensive Japanese dishes are accompanied by good music.

*Paras* is well known for its good Indian food, particularly the chicken curry, biriyani and keema. Although it is not frequented by many westerners those who do venture in usually praise the food quality. This restaurant has been open for more than ten years.

The Taoist symbol hanging outside identifies the *Yin Yang* at Basantapur Square on the fringes of Freak Street. You take off your shoes and sit on the floor in this atmospheric restaurant. Tankas on the wall and photos of Hindu and Buddhist deities add to the mood as does the excellent selection of music. The chop suey and vegetable rolls are particular favourites here.

The *Swiss Restaurant*, is located a block south-west of Durbar Square. Although it can be crowded and the service variable the french fries are generally thought to be the best in Kathmandu. Their goulash, desserts and coffee are also very popular. The *Hotel Lhotse* does good chicken and also serves some typical Nepali dishes like Alu Tama and a salad they dub "Kathmandu Salad". *New Star Italian Restaurant* serves spaghetti and lasagna which have been popular not only with tourists but also long term residents in Kathmandu.

### Low Priced Restaurants

Some of the best gastronomic experiences in Kathmandu can be sampled very cheaply at restaurants in this category. In particular several of the restaurants in the low price range serve excellent Tibetan food you'd have difficulty finding anywhere else in the world.

The *Utse Restaurant* in the Thamel area is, for the price, one of the best restaurants for Chinese and Tibetan food. Its clientele includes not only the budget tourists but also more affluent ones and even some permanent foreign residents. During peak hours it can be so crowded that you may end up sharing a table. Overland bus travellers and voluntary workers are particularly fond of this restaurant. Chinese chow mein, sweet and sour dishes and the Tibetan kothe or momo are all deservedly popular. For Rs 75 you, and three friends, can sample a Tibetan soup, vegetable and meat dish known as Gyatok. Or for Rs 5.25 try the *Utse*'s excellent banana split, their ice cream is very good. A particularly recommended restaurant.

*Mom's Health Food* is on the street with the tree off New Road. It serves health food similar to that in vegetarian restaurants that have sprung up recently in many western countries. Soyaburgers at Rs 4, enchiladas, soups, vegetable or fruit juices and excellent bread are all popular attractions. Nothing spicy here and you get honey instead of sugar in your tea.

> For health food fanatics . . . the only place in Nepal which has real whole wheat bread. The food is just as wholesome and tasy as the health food restaurants in California.
>
> *Carol Pietsch, USA*

The present owner of *Aunt Jane's Place* used to work for the US AID office in Nepal. The original Aunt Jane was the wife of a former director of the Peace Corps in Nepal. Situated one block from Freak Street you have to climb stairs to the first floor to find the clean and typically American food. Often packed with young travellers this restaurant serves renowned chocolate cake, brownies, pies and ice cream. At breakfast time pancakes top the bill.

Another first-floor restaurant is the *Unity* one block back from New Road on the other side. Madan, the long-haired Nepali manager, specialises in American food and serves up one of the best (and safest) salads in Kathmandu. Roast chicken, which comes with boiled vegetables and salad for just Rs 12, is a favourite and the chocolate cake and ice cream makes a good follow up.

In the late sixties the *Peace Restaurant* was the only restaurant in Kathmandu serving good Chinese food. If Mr Wong, the Chinese owner, is around you can be sure that the food will be excellent. It has been renamed *Canton Restaurant-Wong's Kitchen* and it is situated in Lazimpat near the French Embassy. A little off the beaten track, so less likely to be crowded. Right across the street is the *Ringmo Restaurant* where the Chinese and Tibetan food is relatively inexpensive.

On the ground floor of the popular Kathmandu Guest House is the equally popular *Astha Mangalam Restaurant*. Here you can dine on Tibetan or Chinese food surrounded by some of the best decor in Kathmandu. The walls are painted with Tibetan murals, hung with Tankas and you sit on Tibetan rug-covered cushions at elaborately painted tables.

There are several other popular Tibetan restaurants which have been recently opened. *Tso Ngon Restaurant* serves good chow mein and kothe; find it beside the Annapurna Hotel. Back in downtown Kathmandu the *Moti Mahal* with its good Indian tandoori dishes, and the *Cock's Crow Restaurant* are both popular.

Near the Thamel area in Chetrapati you can find the *Snowman Restaurant* which is patronised by many local Tibetans as well as travellers who live in the area. Another Freak Street place is the *Kimling Restaurant* which serves up good Chinese dishes. Among the newly opened restaurants *An An* near the Post Office provides good Chinese food. Try their chop suey.

*K.C.'s Restaurant* in Thamel started by a long haired, bearded Nepalese named Kaysee has become very popular recently for serving good steaks and is crowded by budget travellers and tourists alike. *Bistro Restaurant,* also a recent addition in the same area, serves clean food of good quality. *Nankha Dhing Restaurant* in Thamel has good momos and serves a Tibetan beer called *chang* — Rs 4 a bottle. *Om Restaurant* on the way to Freak Street from New Road serves good Tibetan and Chinese food. Finally you can crowd into the *Cafe De Park* at lunchtime to eat buff hamburgers at Rs 2.75, hot dogs at Rs 3, pizza slices for Rs 4, or try the pies, cakes and coffee. This place reminds me of an American college grill.

## Rock Bottom Restaurants

It is wise to be careful in restaurants in this category although the ones listed here are adequately clean. There are also many good tea stalls and shops in this same price range that may not even have a name. The most popular meal in this group is probably dal bhat tarkari, the rice, dal and vegetable everyday meal of the vast majority of Nepalese. Most of the westerners you find in these places are overland travellers who have been exposed to this kind of food for months and are quite used to it.

The *Mysore Coffee House* is adjacent to the American Library and serves good quality south Indian food. You can try masala dosa here for just Rs 2 or for Rs 5 have a full dinner including rice, chapati, curd and four different kinds of dal and vegetables. This place is also frequented by many budget-conscious Nepali intellectuals.

In the heart of Freak Street the *Golden Dragon Restaurant* is popular with many budget travellers for its Tibetan and Chinese food. The *United Restaurant* is another very inexpensive Freak Street dive, this time the menu is Tibetan and western. It is crowded all day long with cost-conscious travellers many of whom speak highly of the Italian spaghetti and the mashed potatoes.

Still on Freak Street another crowded and popular restaurant rejoices in the name *Eat at Joes.* Amongst the very cheap Chinese dishes you can also find Irish Stew and "Joe's Special". Tibetan and Chinese dishes are again the fare at the long standing *Hungry Eye.* The *Restaurant Stone and Star* in the same building as the Oriental Lodge serves good quality Tibetan food and is packed with young travellers.

The street running down to the river where you find most of the pie shops is also the location for the *Tea Room.* Good music is played throughout the evening and the food is so inexpensive that it has been attracting the low money crowd for nearly a decade. Another ultra low cost eatery is the *Yeti Hotel* — not to be confused with the famous Yak and Yeti. For Rs 3 you can eat as much rice, dai and vegetables as you want.

The *Pleasure Room,* situated just a block from Durbar Square, is a special kind of restaurant. If you are interested in knowing why Nepal was so popular with certain young people until the early seventies then you should visit this place. Good music is played in the evening and one gets the impression that no one there is paying any attention to anyone else. There are many young Nepalese with long hair and a large number of young westerners enjoying the music, atmosphere and the cakes — although it is extremely unlikely that they are "just like your mother makes", as the menu claims!

## Pie Shops and Snackbars

Kathmandu's amazing pie shops are not only one of the most memorable aspects of the city they also have very good pies. Three of the best ones can be found within a few minutes walk from Durbar Square in the street which has been named "Pie Alley" (or less kindly "Pig Alley") by many westerners. The area may not look particularly clean externally but the pie shops themselves are quite clean and their owners usually learnt their pie-making skills while working as domestic helps to Americans in US AID. *New Style Pie Shop* has excellent apple pie, cakes, brownies and cinnamon rolls — more than ten different kinds of pie in all. The *Chi and Pie* is the oldest pie shop in Kathmandu and can offer fifteen different flavours; lemon meringue is the most popular. The best place to eat pies in Freak Street is *Kathmandu Pie Shop* opposite the United Restaurant. *Jamaly Restaurant* in Thamel also serves excellent cakes and pies. The pie shops are especially crowded in the evenings and a popular meeting place for overlanders whose paths last crossed Istanbul or Kabul.

> One of the most pleasant and surprising aspects of Kathmandu is the interesting people one meets in the small restaurants and pie shops. This easygoing exchange of information seems more prevalent here than in most other cities on the way to the east.
>
> *Jim Wanless, USA*

If you want the surroundings to look a little cleaner then head for the *Krishna Loaf Store* near the entrance to the *Yak and Yeti* at Kamal Pokhari. You can get excellent cakes, bread and rolls here. In Thamel *K.C.'s Place* is run by a friendly Nepali named Kaysee who speaks some German. He serves up sheesh kebabs and a variety of cakes to a steady stream of young travellers.

Milk, butter and yak cheese can be bought at the dairy branch on New Road or at the main dairy in Lainchaur near the British Embassy. If you are going trekking make sure to take a few kilograms of cheese along. Cheese costs Rs 20 per kilo and milk Rs 1.20 per bottle.

If you want to taste the best quality Indian sweets like Rasagoolla and Barfi, try *Gutpa's* in New Road in the same block as the American Cultural Center. The sweets available here are clean. *Mona Lisa* at Basantpur Square has good espresso coffee which is quite a rarity in Kathmandu.

## Eating and Drinking Do's and Don'ts

The season you are in Nepal determines whether you need to be very careful or just careful about the water you drink and the food you eat. During the dry tourist season from November to April you could drink tap water in Kathmandu although it is definitely not advisable. During the wet monsoon season from May through September you should always insist on drinking boiled and filtered water. Lack of care can result in diarrhoea, dysentry or even hepatitis but restaurants always boil and filter the water as a matter of course. Remember that tea is always boiled and, therefore, always safe.

When trekking the quality of the water is the single most important cause of stomach disorders. The golden rule is to only drink water from fountains when you are positive that there is no human habitation upstream and to avoid drinking flowing water from rivers or streams. It is still better to boil and filter the water if possible. Above 1500 m you need to be less careful than in the hotter climate at low altitudes.

It is generally quite safe to drink the Tibetan beer known as *chang* which is available very cheaply at places along many of the trekking routes or at Bodhnath and other locations in the valley. It is wise to avoid eating ice cream or any foodstuff which is exposed to the open, particularly from street vendors but in respectable restaurants ice cream is OK.

If you have any doubts about the quality of meat available in an unfamiliar restaurant then try to order egg dishes instead. Avoid eating meat while trekking unless you are carrying your own canned food or if you are certain that the chicken or goat has been freshly slaughtered.

**Stomach Upsets:** If you are unfortunate enough to develop stomach problems in Nepal the best cure is to avoid solid food, drink only hot tea and let your body fight it naturally. If you decide to give it some help Lomotil and Mexaform tablets are both available in pharmacies in Kathmandu.

### Popular Nepalese Food

*chang*— a mild alcoholic beverage made from barley, similar to western style beer.

*thupka* — Tibetan soup containing different kinds of meat.

*momo or kothe*— the Tibetan equivalent of ravioli or dimsims, consists of meat enclosed in dough then steamed or fried.

*dal bhat tarkari* — the typical Nepali meal consisting of lentil soup, rice and curried vegetables

*sikarni* — a sweet dessert made from curd

*gundruk* — a typical Nepalese soup made from dried vegetables.

*tama* — a dried bamboo shoot soup popular in Nepal.

*buff* — since Hindus can't eat beef, buff (water buffalo) is the normal substitute on many menus — buff steaks, buff noodle soup, even buffburgers.

If you develop a taste for chang and would like to brew some up at home here's the recipe. Get a 5 or 10 gallon fermenting vessel from a brewery supply shop. For the smaller vessel boil about 2 kg of millet for several hours. Millet swells considerably so make sure it has plenty of water and doesn't stick. When it cools add water to liquify it, you can also pass it through a blender to smooth it out. Then add burgundy yeast and the juice of a lemon and leave to ferment. This can take several weeks or a couple of months depending on taste. If you like a little extra kick to your chang add sugar, several kg, to the fermenting brew — this is really cheating since in Nepal sugar would be too expensive to be used this way. The final product will have to be strained through a cloth and racked to remove the yeasty taste. This should not be taken as the only way to produce chang — experiment with it; in Bhutan for example they drink a chang made from half millet and half rice.

*recipe from Karel Tiller, Australia*

Honey is available in a shop behind the Ason temple in old Kathmandu. A small jar costs Rs 4 or an 800 gm jar costs about Rs 12. Both whipped honey and cream honey can be purchased and it was the best we found east of Istanbul.

*Jane Arnold and Rellie Lawyer, USA*

## THINGS TO BUY AND WHERE TO BUY THEM

Many different souvenirs and handicrafts can be purchased in Nepal but it is important to shop around. Many items, such as the Tibetan and Chinese wood block prints, were not available at all in the late sixties but now are found in all the new shopping areas. Only Government Emporiums and a very few shops have fixed prices so the golden rule to remember when shopping is bargain! Usually the price first quoted will have a built-in bargaining margin.

Popular buys include:

**Masks:** Paper mache masks of many different sizes are used for mask dancing which takes place in Kathmandu in September. Mask images include elephant headed Ganesh, the terrifying Bhairab and the living Goddess Kumari. Almost all the souvenir shops in Kathmandu sell masks but the best place to buy them inexpensively is the small town of Thimi where they are actually made. Thimi is midway between Kathmandu and Bhaktapur; you can visit the mask painter Kansa Chitrakar on the old Kathmandu to Bhaktapur road about fifteen minutes' walk from the bus stop. Prices range from Rs 5 to 30 depending on size, they make good wall decorations.

**Nepali Caps:** All Nepalese officials are required to wear Nepali caps, topi, when formally dressed, they're black in colour and made in Bhaktapur. Caps are a popular purchase because they look so typically Nepali. There is a cluster of shops selling nothing but caps in an area of old Kathmandu between Asan and Indrachok; prices run from Rs 15 to 20.

**Tibetan Handicrafts:** Tibetan prayer wheels are possibly the best known Tibetan handicraft, they make good presents to take home. Also popular are musical instruments, charm boxes, dorjes (thunderbolts) and other religious items. Bodhnath used to be a good place for Tibetan items but the large number of short-stay tourists who now rush out there on guided tours and indiscriminately buy anything at the first price asked have pushed prices up to absurd levels.

prayer wheel

**Tankas:** Colour paintings of the deities called tankas are painted by Tibetans or by Newars and Tamangs. Many are kept in monastaries but many of the *antique* tankas for sale in Kathmandu are artificially aged over a smoky fire. Tankas can be found for as little as Rs 50 while a good old one could easily cost over Rs 1000. There is no particular place to look for tankas although you will find many in shops at Bodhnath, around Freak Street and in Bhaktapur. At Cheez Beez Bhandar you can see new tankas being painted.

**Nepalese Handicrafts:** Patan, where many traditional handicrafts and bronzeworks are manufactured, is the best place to go. There are now many small shops around Durbar Square in Patan. You can see handicrafts being made at the Patan Industrial Estate at Lagankhel, the prices here are quite low. The Government Emporium on New Road, Kathmandu, also charges fair, fixed prices but the choice is somewhat limited.

> For good bargains in Nepalese or Tibetan curios go to the vendors who spread their wares on blankets in Basantapur or Durbar Square — but be prepared to bargain.
>
> *Stephen Frantz, USA*

**Tibetan Carpets, Jackets, Bags:** It is a good idea to visit the Tibetan refugee camp in Jawlakhel near Patan to see Tibetan carpets being woven. They are also available in the complex of narrow streets between Asan and the National Theatre. A recently opened shop, *Himalayan Handicrafts and Carpets,* in Bijeshwari on the way to the temple of Swayambhu from old Kathmandu has a good selection of carpets. The carpets cost usually from $US80 to 100 each. Their quality is usually better if wool from the highlands (Tibetan wool), is used. The carpets can be vacuumed, although you should ensure that the dyes are colourfast before buying. Tibetan carpets are vibrantly coloured and have striking designs but were originally meant as wall hangings rather than floor coverings. The small square carpets are usually made into seat cushions. The wool jackets, popularly known as *yakets* seem to be worn by every visitor to Kathmandu.

**Block Prints:** Block prints of Tibetan, Chinese and Nepalese deities are available in large numbers printed on local rice paper. Many shops around Freak Street sell prints at prices from Rs 5 to Rs 20 but one of the best places to go is the *Print Shop* next to the Mandarin Restaurant. If you climb up the narrow steps you will find Steve and Christine, an American couple who will answer any questions and show you around the shop.

**Beads:** Married Nepalese women always wear these traditional beads and they make an attractive reminder of Nepal. You can find them at the old bazaar in Bhaktapur or at Asantole in old Kathmandu.

I would recommend a visit to the bead bazar within the main bazar northeast of the Durbar Square. Here you can buy strings of many coloured beads very cheaply and also several thicknesses of materials to make rings and bracelets.

*Annette Mahoney, England*

**Khukris:** The Nepalese knife, traditional weapon of Gurkha soldiers, can be bought for Rs 20 to Rs 500 depending on size and quality.

khukri

**Nepalese Tea:** Tea is grown in Nepal in the far east of the country in the area bordering Darjeeling, it is claimed to equal the famous Darjeeling tea in quality. The best known teas are *Ilam* and *Mountain Gold*, packets of which can be bought for about Rs 15.

**Clothes:** Western women often like Tibetan and Nepalese garments and the *Tantra Boutique*, a block from New Road in the street with the tree, will tailor-make clothes. Laxmi, the lady in the shop, is originally from Darjeeling and speaks good English. The traditional Nepalese coats, overlapping at the front and closed with four ties, are another popular purchase — especially in the maroon velvet material from Pokhara.

**Jewellery:** Jewellery of high and low quality is cheap to buy in Kathmandu and designs and carvings can be created to order.

It will cost you very little to have a Nepalese jeweller working on the street make some article in silver or stone.

*BB, France*

**Terra Cotta:** A wide variety of attractive terra cotta pots, bowls and flowerpots are made — those shaped like an elephant are favourites.

Several shops near Indrachowk sell them, they are made in Thimi.

**Other:** The latest buys include lamp shades of different forms and Batik paintings available in Freak Street which were not common before.

If time permits during your stay in Kathmandu you should visit *Cheez Beez Bhandar*, the shop in Kamal Pokhari near the Yak and Yeti Restaurant. The whole of a fine old Nepali house has been converted into a shop which was originally started by the late Jane Martin, well known for her Aunt Jane's Place Restaurant. Even if you aren't buying it is an interesting place to visit and you'll be certain of seeing many things you'll not have noticed elsewhere in town. You can see tankas being painted here, baskets, costing from Rs 5 upwards, made in southern Nepal, the painted umbrellas used in Nepalese weddings and wooden jewellery boxes.

Nepal is having, in common with many other Asian countries, a major problem of theft of works of art from temples and monasteries. Many of these masterpieces end up in museums or private collections in America or Europe. If you visit Dhulikhel you can walk down to the temple at the foot of the hill and see the three small pairs of feet that are all that remain of the statues which used to stand in the temple.

Should you buy a work of art which could be more than one hundred years old it is necessary to get the permission of the Department of Archaeology before you take it out of the country. If in doubt check — the office is in the National Archives Building (tel 12778), just two blocks from Immigration. Hours are 10 am to 5 pm but if you go around 1 pm you can expect approval by the same evening. To be on the safe side go there a few days before you depart, customs checks are much more severe on exit than entry to the country.

**Getting it all back Home:** Unless you are sure about their reliability it is best not to leave articles to be mailed by the shop where you purchased them. There have been instances when articles have never arrived, unfortunately this is also true of some packing companies — I recommend *Sharma and Sons Packers and Movers* in Kantipath (tel 12709).

## CULTURE

### Cultural Programmes

Even if your visit to Nepal is not during the festival season you can still enjoy Nepalese dance and music in Kathmandu. At the National Theatre there are Nepalese operas and musicals almost every day. In addition programmes of folk dancing are put on by:

*Everest Cultural Society* (tel 15429) shows Nepalese folk dances every evening at 7pm, the one-hour show costs Rs 25. The dances take place in the extravagantly Victorian "hall of mirrors" in the same old Rana palace as the Yak and Yeti Restaurant. Dances from the Sherpa highlands, from the Newars of the valley and from other ethnic groups are shown, including the Yak dance, Peacock dance, Mask dance and Witch Doctor dance.

*Lalupate* (tel 11211) present Nepalese folk dances from a variety of ethnic groups at 6.30 pm in the Soaltee Oberoi Hotel, admission is Rs 20. Every evening at 6.30 pm is also the time for the *Chimal Cultural Group*'s (tel 13471) show at the Manaslu Hotel near the French Embassy.

The *Arnico Cultural Society* (tel 21410), whose nightly show costs Rs 20, went on a three-month tour of England and France in 1975. Their dances take place in Dillibazar; one block from immigration, turn right at the police check post and two more blocks to their building which also contains a small art gallery.

> If you are interested in learning Indian and Nepali classical music, go to Sushma Sada two blocks from Kathmandu Durbar Square (tel 14278). The school gives classes in Kathak, Bharat Natyam (Indian classical) and Chanya (Nepali). You can also contact teachers for tabla, sitar, and mridanga. Students should be prepared to spend at least one month intensively studying; fees are very reasonable.
>
> *Jenny Kerr, Australia*
>
> On Monday nights you can hear the traditional Nepalese music in a temple a few blocks off New Road in Asantol. Wait for the religious ceremony to end at about 9.30 and just sit in the arcade entrance to the temple and watch the warming up of the musicians. It is done with a large chillum and the music begins when the coughing stops.
>
> *Peter Thompson, USA*

## Libraries

Kathmandu has an interesting choice of libraries set up by the Americans, British, French, German, Russian, Chinese and Indians. Not only can you read recent journals, newspapers and books but there are also film nights.

The *French Cultural Centre* (tel 14326) has a good selection of French publications and is open from 3 to 7 pm on weekdays. There are also film nights from Monday to Thursday each week. Membership costs Rs 10 annually or Rs 3 for admission to one film, more than 100 French films are shown during the course of the year. The centre is located near the Leo Hotel in Bagh Bazar.

Located near the post office and the tower, the *Goethe Institute* (tel 15528) has a reading room open from 4 to 7pm daily. Films are shown fairly frequently and there is also an active Nepal-Deutsch club.

The *US Library and Information Service* is on New Road and is open from 11am to 7pm Monday to Friday if you want to keep up with Time and Newsweek. The *British Council* (tel 11305) is on Kantipath and opens from 11am to 6pm Sunday to Friday.

"Rastriya Pustakalaya" or "Nepal National Library" at Pulchok in Patan has books in English, Sanskrit and Indian languages. A large number of the books in the library were collected by the Royal Preceptor in Nepal who had been awarded the title of "jewel of head of scholars" by the King of Nepal. The Tribhuvan University Library at Kirtipur has a nice collection of books and resembles a library in an American university. It is open Sunday to Friday from 9am to 6pm.

The Kaiser Library, near the new Royal Palace, has an incredible collection of books, many on Buddhism, Tibet and Nepal that I have never seen before.

*Hester Ross, USA*

## Research Work

If you are undertaking research on economic, social, and anthropological aspects of Nepal, the best place to contact is the International Research and Consulting Centre, PO Box 1577, Kathmandu. You can also phone Mr Sharad Sharma on 13438.

## Yoga

If you want to learn Yoga while in Kathmandu, there is a place called Arogya Ashram (tel 11833) at Maharajgunj near the American Embassy. They teach different postures (including standing on the head) and "Pranayama".

## Learning Nepali

If you want to learn Nepali from the same instructors who teach Peace Corps Volunteers who work in Nepal, contact Mr Cheej Shrestha at Naxal (near the Lhotse Hotel) or telephone him at 12551. The charges are Rs 20 per hour.

## Cinemas

Indian films, usually not subtitled, are the usual cinematic fare in the valley although there are occasional English language films. Kathmandu has three cinemas and there are also cinemas in Patan and Bhaktapur. Admission charges range from Rs 3 to Rs 10.

> If you do not catch one in India, I suggest you see a Hindi movie. Even if you do not understand Hindi it will be an interesting, artistic experience. The nicest theatre is near the Palace and Chinese Embassy, price is less than Rs 4.
>
> *Bill Cook, USA*

## Media

The *Rising Nepal* is the main English language daily and covers most news from abroad but can be difficult to find if you don't get hold a copy early in the morning. *Radio Nepal* has English news bulletins at 8am and 8.30pm daily. Time and Newsweek are readily available in Nepal. You can buy the latest issues at the store opposite the big tree in New Road.

## Bookshops

Kathmandu has a surprising variety of quite good bookshops with particularly interesting selections of books on Nepal — many of which are not available outside the country. There are bookstalls in the main hotels, in old Kathmandu and around Freak Street. Probably the best selection of books in Kathmandu is at *Educational Enterprises* near New Road Gate or *Ratna Pustak Bhandar* at Asan Tole.

> Visit the Chinese book store located in the bazaar area off Indrachowk. They have beautifully illustrated story books and water colour prints, some in English. They also have interesting sets of post cards, reprints of water colour paintings, glimpses of cities, at an extraordinarily cheap price. Ask to see all the different photos of Mao.
>
> *Kathleen Bannon, USA*

## Night Life in Kathmandu

Many restaurants and snack bars in Kathmandu are so crowded that they make good places to meet Nepalese and other westerners but there are few discos or night clubs as they are known in the west. In Kathmandu, people go to bed quite early and in winter you hardly see anyone on the streets after 10 pm. Besides, many visitors are not particularly worried by the lack of night life, it's not what they have come this far for — so the many places that have opened in the past few years have not all had a long or successful life. For most people a German visitor's comments sum it up: "If you want night life in Kathmandu, you have to make your own." Nevertheless, there are some places:

> The Soaltee Oberoi Casino — for something to do at night. Black Jack, pontoon and a roulette wheel — you might even come away a few rupees richer. Even if you do not like gambling the music is good and it is fun to watch.
>
> *Susan Culkina, USA*

There are free buses to the casino from all the leading hotels of Kathmandu from 8 to 11pm. If you gamble, free drinks are also served. Some hotels also distribute $US5 coupons free which can be exchanged to play at the casino. It is one of the very few casinos in this part of the world. You can play in Indian Rs or $US and take the money out of the country if you win.

There is band music and ballroom dancing at the *Rose Room* of the *Soaltee Oberoi Hotel* almost every evening. The *Footappers* is a new disco which is located away from the city centre of Kathmandu. Taxis from the centre cost about Rs 10. The admission charge is Rs 20 for men and free for women.

# Getting Around

**FLYING**

Royal Nepal Airlines operate a number of scheduled and charter flights around the country. Aircraft used are Avro 748s on the major routes and short take off and landing — STOL, Twin Otters and Pilatus Porters to the smaller places — mainly for trekkers. These trekking flights are not scheduled but during the trekking season departures are frequent and tickets can be obtained from the trekking agents. RNAC also operate Bell Helicopters which give a tremendous view of the country but at quite high cost.

### Regular Destinations:
**Central Nepal** — Baglung, Bhairawa, Bharatpur, Gorkha, Janakpur, Jomosom, Pokhara, Rumjatar, Simra
**Western Nepal** — Dang, Dhangadi, Jumla, Nepalganj, Rukumkot, Sanfe Bagar, Silgarhi Doti, Surkhet
**Eastern Nepal** — Bhadrapur, Biratnagar, Lamidanda, Rajbiraj, Taplejung, Tumlingtar

**Charter Destinations**   the following are the main destinations for trekking flights, remember you are only allowed 10 kg of baggage on these small aircraft.

**Lukla or Syangboche** — 45 and 50 minutes flight from Kathmandu in the Solu Khumbu region on the route to Everest.
**Langtang** — 25 minutes north of Kathmandu.
**Dhorpatan** — 90 minutes west in the Dhaulagiri mountain range area.
**Jumla** — 120 minutes east on the route to Rara Lake.
**Jomosom** — 60 minutes flight east towards the Annapurnas.

**Helicopter Charter** — RNAC operate a number of set tours in their helicopters at a cost of $US375 per hour. The popular destinations include the Helambu district, north-east of Kathmandu; the Langtang Valley; the Everest region far to the east and Lumbini, Buddha's birthplace, near the Indian border to the south-west. As the seating capacity of a helicopter is four or five persons the cost per person per hour is about $US75. Approximate flying times for some well known destinations are:

| | | |
|---|---|---|
| Kathmandu | —Helambu | 35 minutes |
| Kathmandu | — Everest | 2 hours |

| Kathmandu | — Lumbini | 3 hours |
| Kathmandu | — Gorkha | 1 hour |

## GUIDED TOURS

Travel agencies in Kathmandu organise scheduled conducted tours and private tours by car or coach to places of touristic interest. If your stay in Nepal is too short to permit exploration on your own, then it is best to join a conducted or private tour.

*Everest Travel* conducts a Rs 40 tour to the Durbar Squares of the three cities of Kathmandu Valley each Monday and Thursday morning. A conducted tour to Nagarkot on Monday, Thursday and Saturday to watch the sunset and sunrise over the world's highest peaks cost Rs 90 per person including overnight accommodation. On Wednesday and Sunday afternoons they run conducted tours to the temples of Pashupatinath, Bodhnath and Bhaktapur for Rs 40.

*Kathmandu Travel* has conducted tours to Pashupatinath, Bodnath and Bhaktapur on Monday, Thursday, and Friday mornings for Rs 40. Tours to Kathmandu City, Swayambhunath and Patan on Monday, Wednesday, Thursday and Friday afternoons cost Rs 35. On Tuesday and Sunday mornings there is a Rs 60 tour to watch the sunrise on Everest.

These agencies and others such as *Yeti Travels, Third Eye Travels* and *Gorkha Travel* will also arrange private tours if requested, at widely differing prices. Most agencies will arrange tours to Budhanilkantha to see the sleeping Vishnu. *Kathmandu, Gorkha* and *Shankar Travel* all arrange tours to the temple of Changunarayan. Almost all the agencies organise a trip to Dhulikhel along the road to the Chinese border and to the border itself. Some agencies, like *Kathmandu Travel* for Rs 44, organise conducted tours to the temple of Daxinkali to watch the animal sacrifices on Tuesday and Saturday mornings. Occasionally overland bus companies will use their vehicles for tours during the periods between their trips.

## DO-IT-YOURSELF TRANSPORT

Cars can be hired through *Yeti Travels* or *Gorkha Travels* in Kathmandu but the cost is fairly high both in terms of initial hiring charge and the high cost of fuel — over $US2 per gallon. Taxis, on the other hand, are quite reasonably priced — any ride around town should come to less than Rs 10 and a taxi can be hired all day for Rs 100 to 150. A group of people can tour the valley quite cheaply by taxi. A number of garages, particularly around Freak Street, hire out motorcycles by the day or week but at about Rs 150 per day they are also quite expensive.

Bicycle rickshaws only cost Rs 2 to Rs 5 for any ride around town but be certain to agree a price before you start. For the fit and healthy bicycle hire is the ideal way to get around — the valley is sufficiently compact and flat to make riding a pleasure. Daily hire charges vary from Rs 3 to 5; get up early for the best selection of bikes and make sure you lock it when leaving it.

> To discover the Kathmandu Valley with its three cities there is no better way than by bicycle, it costs less than Rs 5 a day and they can be hired in different places around the city.
>
> *Joelle Lambelle, France*

**but**

> if you do not like bicycles the bus service is inexpensive and well organised but during the monsoon enquire about the condition of the roads.
>
> *Genette Katz and Nadine Cals, France*

## PUBLIC TRANSPORT

Bus travel around Kathmandu and the valley is very cheap although often equally crowded. Less sardine like but also inexpensive are the smaller mini-buses and the curious little three-wheeler tempos. The three main bus stations are all situated around the parade ground.

**Post Office and Martyr's Gate:** Buses and tempos to Patan.
**Bhimsen Tower near the Post Office:** Buses to Pokhara and the Indian border.
**Bagh Bazar, near the Park and Clock Tower:** Buses east to Bhaktapur.
**City Hall:** Buses to Pokhara, Janakpur and the Indian border, Dhulikhel and points along the road to the Chinese border, Kakarbitta (eastern border of Nepal near Darjeeling).
**Opposite the park near the clock tower:** Buses to Bodnath, Kirtipur, Pashuputinath and Patan.

**Balaju, Lazimpat and Maharajgunj:** Tempos leave from the same National Theatre location for these three places and charge 75 paisa. Many of the embassies are located in Maharajgunj.

**Patan:** Buses leave along the park near the clock tower, they depart every fifteen minutes and charge 50 paisa. Tempos depart from the Post Office and the park beside the Clock Tower, as soon as they have six passengers, cost 75 paisa and take just ten minutes to reach Patan.

**Bhaktapur:** Buses leave every twenty minutes between 6am and 8pm from the stop across Durbar Marg from the Park Restaurant. The regular buses cost 75 paisa while the faster and more comfortable minibuses charge Rs 1. You can also get to Bhaktapur by the new trolleybus service which runs from the statue at Tirprusewar through Thimi to the outskirts of Bhaktapur for 50 paisa. It is a fifteen minute walk from the trolleybus terminal to the city centre in Bhaktapur.

**Budhanilkantha:** Buses to the sleeping Vishnu leave from the National Theatre near the lake and charge Rs 1.50 or you can travel by tempo for Rs 2.

**Daxinkali:** Buses to the temple of Daxinkali where animal sacrifices are performed, leave from near the park and the Clock Tower on Tuesday and Saturday mornings.

**Dhulikhel and along the Chinese border road to Lamosangu:** Buses to these places leave from the big bus terminal near the City Hall. There are departures almost every hour for Dhulikhel or Banepa and the fare to Dhulikhel is Rs 2.50. Buses to Barabise or Lamosangu out towards the Chinese border depart at 6am, 10am and 2pm.

**Pokhara:** Buses leave in the early morning near the Post Office or at the big bus park near the City Hall. It is advisable to reserve seats and buy tickets at least a day in advance.

**Indian Border:** Buses to Birganj and Raxaul or to Janakpur and the eastern border near Darjeeling can be found at the City Hall bus park.

**Bodhnath:** Minibuses charge 80 paisa to Bodhnath and leave from in front of the Park Restaurant, they depart when full. Pashupatinath is an intermediate point and the name of the stop is Gosala.

**Kirtipur and the University:** Buses charge 40 paisa and leave every fifteen minutes from the Park Restaurant, there are also mini-buses.

**Godavari:** To go to the botanical garden take a bus to Lagankhel and change.

**Trisuli:** To reach this starting point for the Langtang trek go to the main dairy at Lainchaur near the British Embassy. Walk three blocks west on the road leading in that direction until you reach the bus station known as Sorakutte Pati, buses also leave here for Kakani.

# Seeing the Valley

## KATHMANDU VALLEY

If you arrive by air the Kathmandu Valley will be the first place you visit in Nepal. As far as art and architecture are concerned your visit to Nepal need go no further than the valley. Three important cities stand in the valley, the most important being Kathmandu itself. Patan, the most "Buddhist" of the three is across the Bagmati River to the south of Kathmandu but so close as to be almost an extension of the capital. It is known to this day for its excellent works of art and carvings in wood and bronze. Bhaktapur, also known as Bhadgaon, is the most "medieval" of the three and is situated in the eastern part of the valley. While Kathmandu and Patan have undergone great changes in the two decades since Nepal ended its long isolation, Bhaktapur has changed very little and is still much as it was two decades ago, some would say three centuries.

Kathmandu stands at about 1350 m and the valley is surrounded by hills whose altitude is around 2400 m. The original inhabitants of the valley were a people known as the Newars and they still form a majority of the population. Typical Newar towns in the valley are Thimi, Bode, Chapagaon — south of Patan and Sankhu. There has also been much migration from other parts of the country, mainly by Brahmins and Chetris who can be found in suburban areas of Kathmandu and Patan, and in villages to the western side of the valley. Many of the people living in the hills surrounding the valley are Tamangs.

Until Nepal's unification process from small principalities and kingdoms started two hundred years ago there were small independent kingdoms in the valley. The kingdoms of Kathmandu, Bhaktapur and Patan all had amazingly sophisticated art and architecture, especially during the 17th century which was the golden age for the construction of temples and palaces in the three cities. It makes a romantic picture to think of these three medieval kingdoms nestled in a fertile valley in the Himalayas — sometimes fighting each other but more often celebrating numerous feasts and festivals and competing in the building of temples and other works of art. At this same time temples and idols were being indiscriminately destroyed in India. The affluence of the valley was assured by its strategic position on a major trade route between Tibet and the north Indian plains. The kings in the valley were sometimes Hindu and sometimes Buddhist.

Then in 1768 King Prithvi Narayan Shah started his campaign to unify Nepal. The three kings of the valley were defeated and the foundations of a united Nepal were laid. The use of the Nepali language, a member of the Indo-European family of languages, replaced the Tibeto-Burmese Newari language of the valley as the language of administration.

Today the valley is the most developed part of Nepal with a network of roads and electricity in most of the villages. The availability of improved seeds, fertilizers and extensive irrigation has allowed the farmers to cultivate wheat as well as the traditional rice. Two decades ago rice was often the only crop. Land reform programmes have allowed the farmer a larger share of produce which once had to be given to the landlords.

## KATHMANDU

Kathmandu is both the capital of Nepal and the largest city in the country. Most of the interesting things to see in Kathmandu are clustered in the old part of town between the old market place and the new shopping area along New Road. Around the central Durbar Square are the old Royal Palace, a number of interesting pagoda and Indian style temples and the Kumari Devi, residence of the living goddess. Some of the interesting things to see in the Durbar Square area include:

Black Bhairab

**Kalo Bhairab** (39) This huge stone image of the terrifying Black Bhairab was once used as a form of lie detector. Suspected wrongdoers were forced to touch the feet of the god and swear whether they had committed the crime. It was said that lying brought immediate death!

Road, Freak Street and Durbar Square today, and far over the valley. The courtyard next to the white building to the southeast has a small temple where Malla kings, whose bodies were not taken to the burning ghats on the Bagmati, were cremated.

**King Pratap Malla** (32) The statue of the king sitting with folded hands surrounded by his four sons on top of a pillar facing the palace temple is supposed to be this most famous Malla king.

**Drums and Bell** (13) The giant drums are across the road next to the police station and were built in the 18th century as was the bell which followed sixty years after the similar bells in Patan and Bhaktapur. Usually a new and unique addition to one of the valley towns' Durbar Squares at that time was immediately copied by the others!

**Kumari Devi** (9) The three-storey building with the artistic windows looking out on to Durbar Square, its door guarded by stone lions, is the Kumari Devi — house of the living goddess. The continued veneration of a young girl, as if she were a real goddess, is part of the magic that makes Kathmandu a real "living museum".

The big gate beside the Kumari Devi conceals the huge chariot which takes the Kumari around the city of Kathmandu once a year. Entering the house you reach a courtyard surrounded by balconies with 18th century masterpieces of woodcarving. Perhaps you might catch a glimpse of the goddess in the windows, she is a young girl and easily recognisable by the black shadowing around her eyes which extends as far as her ears and by her hair which is piled up over her head. Photographing her is not allowed. The courtyard contains a miniature stupa with a symbol of Saraswati the goddess of learning on its side, looking like a star of David, and a mandala on a lotus. Non-Hindu or Buddhist people are not allowed to go beyond this courtyard.

A   Peacock window in Bhaktapur
B   Temple strut at Changunarayan
C   Bodhnath stupa

Kumari

The Kumari is not born a goddess nor does she remain one all her life. She is always chosen from a caste of Newar goldsmiths and is usually about five years old, it is essential that she has never been hurt or shed blood. After careful screening by a number of people including the astrologer, the selected candidates, about ten in number, are locked in a dark room where fearful-looking masks and freshly slaughtered buffalo heads are kept. Frightening noises are made from outside and the girl who shows least fear is selected. She is installed on her throne, in the same room where she lives, during the Dasain festival and the spirit of the goddess is said to enter her body after this ceremony. As soon as she reaches puberty the Kumari becomes human once more and a new goddess must be chosen.

For three days each September, during the festival for the God Indra — marking the end of the monsoon season, the Kumari is taken by chariot around Kathmandu. The Kumari also blesses the King of Nepal on this occasion, putting a red tika mark on his forehead and receiving a gold coin in return. It is said that the Kumari gave her blessing to the grandfather of the present King very reluctantly in the year when he was to die. People say that she was feeling very sleepy and had to be literally forced to mark his forehead. The Kumari goes out officially five to six times a year during major festivals including the big and small Dasains in October and April when she appears at the old Royal Palace, Hanuman Dhoka.

The present Kumari was only five years old when she was selected in the early seventies. When she reaches puberty she will return to her parents' home only three blocks from the Kumari Devi. Her expenses are paid by revenue from *Guthi*, the lands under the ownership of temples or deities. These funds provide adequate amounts of rice, salt and dal but meat and firewood have to be purchased separately. The Kumari also gets a considerable sum in offerings from devotees. The Kumari is not supposed to go to school but the last one had a visiting teacher and the present Kumari is also being educated. When she retires she receives a government allowance of Rs 50 a month until she marries when a lump sum of Rs 1000 is paid as dowry. She gets no further allowances after marriage.

There is a popular belief that the man who marries an ex-Kumari may die within six months and should, therefore, be strong both physically and mentally. This could lead, not unexpectedly, to a general reluctance to marry a Kumari but many people now believe this is simply superstition and cite cases of husbands outliving an ex-Kumari.

The institution of the Kumari dates back at least two centuries to the last Malla king of Kathmandu, Jayaprakash Malla. He once had intercourse with a pre-pubescent girl and as a result the young girl later died. The King was then told in his dreams to start the institution of the Kumari, worship her and once each year convey her around Kathmandu as penance for his sins. The institution may have existed even earlier and only the custom of the Kumari visiting the city by chariot started at this time. The last Malla king of Kathmandu was defeated on the day of the Kumari festival and the first king of the present Shah dynasty received his blessing on that same day as was customary.

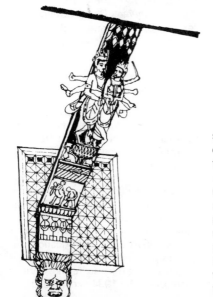

temple strut

**Erotic Carvings:** There are several temples in the square with erotic carvings on the struts but the best carvings are those on the **Jaganath Temple** (33) beside the monkey god Hanuman. There are a number of explanations for the presence of these carvings on so many temples but the most pleasing is that the goddess of lightning is a chaste virgin and would not consider striking a temple with such shocking goings-on.

There are many other interesting sights to see around the Durbar Square apart from the continual bustle of Nepalese life itself. A pleasant hour can easily be spent sitting on the platform of the **Trailokya Mohan Temple** (7) or the **Maju Deval** (10) and watching the flute salesmen, trishaw riders, fruit and vegetable sellers, postcard hawkers and tourists below. The three-roofed **Trailokya Mohan** is easily identified as a temple to Vishnu by the fine Garuda kneeling before it. The large three-roofed **Maju Deval** with its nine-stage platform has some interesting erotic carvings and gives a good view over the square and out to Swayambhunath. From here you can look across to the **Shiva-Parvati Temple** (12) where images of the God and his Goddess look out from the window on the activity below. The white neo-classical building looking highly out of place in the exotic Durbar Square is the **Gaddi Baithak** (8) which was built as a palace during the Rana period.

At the top of Pie Alley, across from the Kasthamandap Temple is the small **Maru Ganesh** (4) temple dedicated to Ganesh and a constant hive of activity — Ganesh is a very popular god. The **Shiva Temple** (3) slightly down from this is used by barbers who can usually be seen squatting on the platform around it. Many of the temples in the square were badly damaged in the 1934 earthquake and have subsequently been restored, rebuilt or modified. An excellent and highly-readable description of the history, significance and architecture of many of the Durbar Square buildings can be found in *An Introduction to Hanuman Dhoka* published by Tribuhuvan University and available very cheaply in Kathmandu.

flute seller

Kathmandu will provide many other interesting sights to the casual wanderer. Set out from the centre and explore the mazed alleys and crowded squares of the market area north of the Durbar Square, you'll find many surprises. The white, minaret-like **Bhimsen Tower** was constructed as a watch tower by a prime minister and is of no particular significance but serves as a useful landmark. It was renovated after suffering serious damage in the 1934 earthquake.

**Durbar Square:** Another five minutes walk brings you to the Durbar Square where the ancient royal palace of Patan is located. The British writer Landon had this to say of the square at the beginning of this century:

> As an ensemble, the Durbar Square of Patan probably remains the most picturesque collection of buildings that has been set in so small a place by the piety and pride of oriental men.

Most of the buildings in the square were built in the 17th century by the famous Malla King of Patan, Siddhinarsingh Malla. The Royal Palace and Taleju Temple stand on the left side of the square while the temple of Krishna and a host of other temples stand on the right. Patan's biggest market place, the Mangal Bazar, is also around the square.

**Bhimsen Temple:** The first temple on the right can be discerned by the pillar with a lion on top in front of it. Bhimsen was a figure from the epic Mahabharata and according to the legend one of the strongest men who ever lived. The three-storied temple has a golden-coloured facade on its first floor.

**Shiva Temple:** The second temple with two stone elephants guarding the door is that of Shiva. Shiva's animal, the bull, is on the other side of the temple. The first floor is quite artistic and there are erotic carvings on the roof support struts.

**Krishna Mandir:** The third temple, dedicated to Krishna, is the most famous in the Durbar Square. Built by King Siddhinarsingh Malla in the 17th century it was influenced by Indian architecture, not the usual pagoda styles. The mythical man-bird Garuda sits with folded hands on top of a pillar since Krishna is the incarnation of Vishnu and the Garuda was his animal. The stone carvings at the top of the first floor pillars tell story of the Mahabharata while the second floor carved scenes come from the Ramayana. A major festival is held here in August on the occasion of Krishna's birthday. A characteristic feature of this temple is that there are no nails or wood and the construction is entirely of stone.

**King Yoganarendra Malla:** This king ruled Patan in the early 18th century and his statue tops the tall pillar. A bird stands on top of the statue and legend says that one day it will fly away.

**Other Temples:** Next to the king is a white Indian style temple and then a Shiva temple of three storeys with many erotic carvings. The big bell beside the Shiva temple was supposed to be rung by people wishing to draw the attention of the king to injustices they were suffering. A small stone temple of Krishna completes the left side of the square.

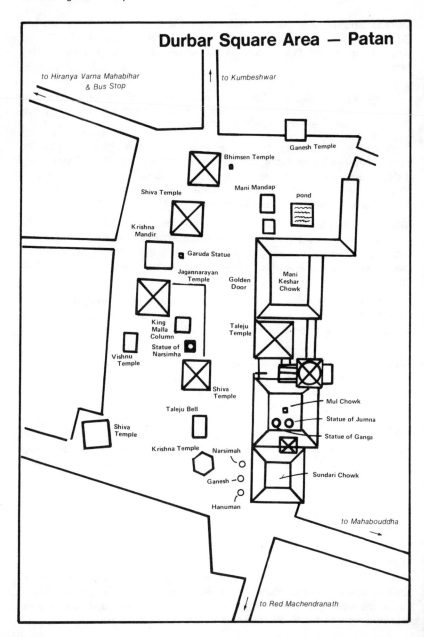

# Durbar Square Area — Patan

to Hiranya Varna Mahabihar
& Bus Stop

to Kumbeshwar

Ganesh Temple

Bhimsen Temple

Shiva Temple

Mani Mandap

pond

Krishna
Mandir

Garuda Statue

Jagannarayan
Temple

Golden
Door

Mani
Keshar
Chowk

King
Malla
Column

Taleju
Temple

Statue of
Narsimha

Vishnu
Temple

Shiva
Temple

Mul Chowk

Statue of Jumna

Statue of Ganga

Taleju Bell

Shiva
Temple

Sundari Chowk

Krishna Temple

Narsimah

Ganesh

Hanuman

to Mahabouddha

to Red Machendranath

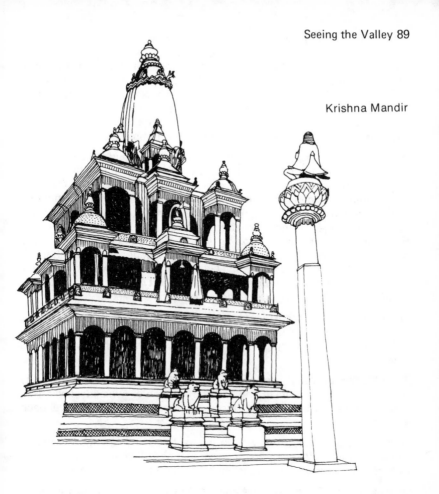

Krishna Mandir

**Water Tap:** Starting again on the right side of the square the big stone water tap is the first thing seen. When the bird atop the king flies off the same legend continues that the stone elephants guarding the entrance to the Shiva temple will walk across to the tap for a drink.

**Royal Palace:** The golden gate and artistic wooden and bronze windows mark the Royal Palace of Patan. In a room in this palace the spirit of one of the Malla kings is supposed to continue to exist; to this day a daily offering of tobacco in a water pipe is made.

**Taleju Temple:** The three-storied temple of the Goddess Taleju was built in the mid 17th century and has excellent wood carvings. If you enter and go into the courtyard you will see a beautiful four-storied pagoda with statues representing Ganga, the River Ganges and Jumna, the River Jumna, guarding the entrance. The main palace is towards the end of the courtyard and outside stand statues of Ganesh, Narsimha and Hanuman. The entrance leads to Sundarichowk or the "beautiful courtyard". There is very beautiful woodwork on the first floor seen from the courtyard and the royal bath with a small replica of the Krishna Temple.

**Mahabouddha Temple:** The temple of one thousand Buddhas is about ten minutes walk south of the Durbar Square. It is slightly out of the way and you may have to ask directions as it is located in a courtyard surrounded by buildings and not easily visible despite its height. Originally constructed in the 14th century, the terra cotta, Indian style temple was severely damaged in the 1934 earthquake and later rebuilt. Each of the bricks in this building contains an image of Buddha. Inside there is a shrine dedicated to Maya Devi, the mother of Buddha. It is said that this temple is similar to the one in Bodh Gaya where Buddha was enlightened. You can climb the buildings around the courtyard to photograph the temple and obtain a fine view over the rooftops of Patan.

**Rudra Varna Mahabihar:** This monastery is situated in a courtyard near the temple of Mahabouddha and is similar to the monastery near the city gate. There are many images of Buddha as well as much artwork on the walls.

**Rato Machendranath:** The temple of Red Machendranath is a little way out from the centre of town and has a fine image of Avalokiteshwar, Red Machendranath, which is taken around the town during his festival each year.

**Ashoka Stupas:** During his visit to the valley 2500 years ago the Indian Buddhist emperor Ashoka erected four stupas indicating the boundaries of Patan. You can see the grassy humps where they once stood.

**Jawlakhel:** The Tibetan refugee camp is only about ten minutes walk from the centre of town, here you can see carpets, rugs and pullovers being made — the camp is closed on Saturdays. Prices may be slightly lower than elsewhere in Kathmandu. The handicrafts centre was set up with Swiss assistance. The only zoo in Nepal is situated close to the camp but is not particularly interesting.

> To visit a typical Newar village go to Chapagaon, south of Jawlakhel. Just take the dirt road and continue walking till you reach a very densely populated village.
>
> *Jane Wolff, USA*

One of the specialities of Bhaktapur is its curd known as *Jujudhau* which means the *king of curds* in Newari. During autumn and winter it is perfectly safe to taste it in one of the several shops recently opened near the bus station.

*Judy Crawford, USA*

**Statue of the Goddess and Bhairab:** If you walk up from the bus stop past the Hindi movie cinema you come to a gate flanked by stone statues. They are considered to be excellent examples of 17th century Nepalese art showing the Goddess Ugrachandi on the left and Bhairab on the right. The Goddess has several hands and is in the process of killing a demon. After producing these statues the poor sculptor had his hands cut off on the orders of the king to prevent him from reproducing these magnificent works.

**Art Gallery:** A few more steps brings you into the Durbar Square of Bhaktapur with the Art Gallery on your left. Admission is only 20 paisa and the gallery contains many rare paintings and manuscripts from medieval Nepal. The paintings showing Hindu and Buddhist styles of Tantrism are particularly interesting as are the fine miniatures and the stone figure of Hari Shankar — half Vishnu and half Shiva.

It is very interesting to watch the potters making pots out of clay. Just wander for about five minutes around Durbar Square and you will come across several potters making different kinds of utensils and pots.

*Heinz Aulenbach, Austria*

**Golden Gate:** Adjoining the gallery is the Golden Gate of Bhaktapur built by the last Malla king in the middle of the 18th century. According to Percy Brown, who visited Nepal in 1912, this was the liveliest work of art in the whole of Nepal. A Garuda, the vehicle of Vishnu, tops the gate and is shown eating serpents, its traditional enemies. The other, multi-headed, figure riding the Garuda is the Goddess Kali.

**Statue of King Bhupatindra:** King Bhupatindra Malla was perhaps the most famous of the Malla kings and was responsible for much of the building and works of art in Bhaktapur in the late 17th century. His image sits with folded hands on the top of the pillar facing the gate. This representation of the king on a pillar and a similar one in Patan were copied from the one in Kathmandu's Durbar Square.

**Fifty Five Windowed Palace:** On the other side of the gate stands the palace which was first constructed in the 15th century and renovated in the late 17th. Opposite the palace is a large bell known as the *barking bell.* King Bhupatindra set it up in the late 17th century to avoid the effects of a bad dream, even today people say that dogs bark and weep when the bell is rung. The Durbar Square also contains a replica of the Pashupatinath Temple, built in the 15th century, with some athletic erotic carvings on the struts.

**Nyatapola Temple:** The five-storied Nyatapola Temple is both the highest temple in the valley and one of the finest examples of Nepalese architecture and craftsmanship. The temple is visible from the Durbar Square and only a short walk away. King Bhupatindra constructed this temple at the beginning of the 18th century and is said to have laid the foundations himself, after which the temple was built in just a few months. The stairway leading to the temple is flanked by two wrestlers, then two elephants, two lions, two griffins and finally two goddesses. Each pair is supposed to be ten times more powerful than the preceding one and even the bottom wrestlers are ten times as strong as any mortal man. One of the finest views of the temple can be had from the road running out of the valley towards the Chinese border. The whole town of Bhaktapur can be seen backed by the mountains and with the five stories of the temple rising majestically over the lesser buildings.

**Bhairabnath Temple:** The two-storied Bhairabnath Temple stands to the right of the Nyatapola and was originally constructed early in the 17th century. It has been rebuilt after suffering severe damage in the 1934 earthquake and is unusual for having a rectangular, not square, base.

**Dattatraya Temple:** Only five minutes walk from the temple of Nyatapola brings you to the square containing the Dattatraya Temple and the Pujahari Math monastery. Built in the 15th century this is the oldest temple in the area and was built for Vishnu; as a Garuda topped pillar and his traditional weapons indicate. The temple is said to 'have been constructed from the wood of a single tree.

Nyatapola temple

**Pujahari Math:** The nearby monastery is equally old and originally served as an inn for pilgrims on the occasion of Sivaratri. A chief monk still lives there. The wooden carvings inside the courtyard are extraordinarily rich but the famous *peacock window*, probably the finest carved window in the valley, should definitely not be missed. The window is in the small alley on the side of the monastery, turn left on leaving the main entrance. The restoration work on the monastery was completed with assistance from West Germany. Further restoration work and the provision of drinking water and sewage facilities to part of Bhaktapur under the Bhaktapur Development Project is also being assisted by West Germany.

## SWAYAMBHUNATH

The Buddhist temple of Swayambhunath, situated on the top of a hillock west of the city, is one of the most popular attractions in Nepal. You can either take a taxi to get there or walk in just twenty minutes from Durbar Square. A useful shortcut is to go down Pig Alley, where the pie shops are located, from the square until you reach the river. Cross by the footbridge and keep on going until you reach the base of the hill, walking up to Swayambhu reminds me somewhat of the Sacre Coeur in Paris.

The stairs leading to the temple from the east are quite steep and you might prefer the gradual climb from the southern part of the hillock where the restaurants are located. The temple has also been called the *Monkey Temple* as there are numerous monkeys roving around the place who thrive on offerings made by the devotees. They will entertain you by sliding down the handrail as you climb the steps.

The ever watchful eyes of Buddha on the central stupa, the countless prayer wheels and the huge thunderbolt (Bajra in Sanskrit or Dorje in Tibetan) at the top of the stairs have long impressed visitors. Beside the stupa there is a large image of Buddha while the pagoda style temple on the north-west side of the stupa contains a beautiful image of the goddess Hariti. She was the goddess of smallpox and used to devour children until Buddha made her stay near him and give up this bad habit. The complex also contains two Indian style temples, giving the visitor a chance to view a wide variety of architectural types. Swayambhunath gives a panoramic view over Kathmandu, particularly striking in the evening when the city is illuminated.

> If you are lucky enough to be in Nepal during a full moon, try to spend part of it right up at Swayambhunath. Be sure to wander round the rear of the main stupa. There are many white stupas that glow peacefully under a full moon.
>
> *John Vogt, USA*

Swayambhunath's stupa is reputed to be the oldest in Nepal. Although the earliest written reference to the place was made in the 13th century, there is little doubt that the site is very old — perhaps as much as 2000 years. Geologists now accept that the Kathmandu Valley was at one time a

The big bull, Shiva's animal, inside the temple was built in the last century. The small bull in front of the temple is about three centuries old. Last year I visited the temple with a minister of the French government, he was so moved by the sight of the temple that he said of it, "there are places like this where the spirit moves".

The best time to visit the temple is on *Ekadashi,* a day which occurs twice each month. On those days there will be many pilgrims and a special ceremony in the evening called *Arati* characterised by the ringing of bells. There many also be devotional music and illuminations. In the month of February there is a big fair at the temple to celebrate Shiva's birthday and another fair takes place in November.

## NEPAL MUSEUM

The Nepal museum is close to Swayambhu and slightly to the south, a convenient visit on the way back to the city. The museum is open daily except Tuesdays from 10.15 to 15.30 in the winter and from 10.30 to 16.30 in the summer. The new building contains many beautiful carvings in wood and some especially interesting bronze idols. The old building illustrates recent Nepalese history with the uniforms and weapons of Nepalese soldiers and generals from the past two centuries. A sword which Napoleon presented to a Nepalese Prime Minister and leather cannons captured during the war with Tibet in 1856 are particular attractions.

## BODHNATH

Bodhnath is one of the biggest stupas in the world and is believed to be at least four or five centuries old. It is located about 8 km from the city, quite close to the airport and the Hindu temple of Pashupatinath. The bones of Kashyapa Buddha, one of the Buddhas who preceded Gautama Buddha, are said to be contained in the stupa. It is possible this stupa was constructed after the introduction of Buddhism in Tibet when relations between Nepal and Tibet were amicable.

Bodhnath is the centre of Tibetan culture in Nepal and you will see many Tibetan refugees here. Chini Lama, the priest of some of the Tibetan Buddhists, lives here and close to the stupa there is also a new Tibetan monastery. The stupa is surrounded by small shops selling Tibetan handicrafts and garments. Nepalese call the village where the stupa is located Bodh. Just north-east of the stupa is a big monastery, "gompa" in Nepali, which is also worth visiting.

The best *chang* in the Kathmandu Valley is available in Bodhnath.
*Marie Claude Virot, France*

Some visitors, deeply interested in Buddhism and meditation, decide to make a prolonged stay at Bodhnath and there are rooms in private homes which can be rented here for as little as Rs 100 per month. About an hour's walk north of Bodhnath is a hillock at Kappan with a Buddhist monastery. A meditation course on Mahayana Buddhism is given annually from the first week of November to December by the monastery's Tibetan and western monks. In 1975 almost all of the 250 participants were westerners. They paid Rs 800 per month for room and board and were supposed to live a life of strict discipline — no smoking or drinking. A two-week course is offered in the spring and there is also the possibility of a retreat. Write for information to:

International Mahayana Institute
PO Box 817,
Kathmandu, Nepal

If you spend even one afternoon talking to the western born Buddhist monks and nuns at Kappan monastery it might change your life. Western students can be found living there year round and rooms are available to those seriously intending to learn.

*George Churinoff, USA*

## CHANGUNARAYAN

The temple of Changunarayan is situated on a hilltop north of Bhaktapur and is sufficiently inaccessible that few visitors make the effort to see it. If you are interested in art and architecture and willing to take a few hours walk in the countryside then you will find a trip to this place very worthwhile. Changunarayan has several masterpieces of 5th and 12th century Nepalese art as well as the oldest stone inscription found in the valley.

It is possible to combine a walking visit to the temple with a trip to the stupa of Bodhnath or the town of Bhaktapur. It is also possible to walk to Changunarayan after watching the sunrise from Nagarkot, the descent to the temple takes about four hours.

To reach Changunarayan from Bhaktapur takes about two hours on foot. The hillock, looking rather like Swayambhu, is visible to the north of Bhaktapur from the bus stop but it is best not to walk directly towards it as the trail is poor. For a better trail walk to the Durbar Square then follow any road heading north. Ten minutes walk through narrow alleys will take you to the northern edge of town where you can see the hill clearly. Simply follow the trail until you reach the bottom of the hill from where it is fifteen minutes steep climb to the top.

The pagoda style temple is dedicated to Narayana or Vishnu. The temple itself is not very old, perhaps two centuries, but the site is at least fifteen centuries old. A garuda, the mythical man-bird mount of Vishnu stands in front of the temple with folded hands. It is supposed to have been set up in the 5th century and is one of the most important attractions in the valley. In front of the statue is the oldest stone inscription in the valley made in Gupta script and dating back to the same century.

The temple is flanked by four pillars topped by the traditional weapons of Vishnu including the lotus and conch. There are a number of images of Vishnu around the courtyard holding these weapons in his four hands. In the north-east corner of the courtyard there is an image of Vishnu riding a gardua, this image is reproduced on the Nepalese Rs 10 note.

The site also contains an image of Vishnu superimposed on top of another image, one of the most picturesque and famous idols in the valley. It is supposed to date back to the 5th or 6th century although half of it is broken. There are a number of other outstanding statues from the 12th and 13th centuries including an image of Narsimha near the entrance. In Sanskrit the word Narsimha means "man and lion" and is supposed to be one of the ten incarnations of Vishnu, in this case half human and half lion. The statue shows Narsimha killing a demon.

There is an interesting legend of how this incarnation took place — a demon pleased Brahma and in return received a promise that he could not be killed by a man or an animal, in day or in night, nor by any weapon. Unfortunately the demon then started terrorising the inhabitants of earth and Vishnu himself had to take this man-lion (neither man nor beast) incarnation and use his nails (which were not a weapon) to defeat the demon in the evening (which was neither day nor night).

After leaving Changunarayan it is a short, steep descent to the river which can be easily crossed by a temporary bridge during the dry season. Two hours walk, passing by the Royal Game Reserve at Gokarna, will take you to the stupa at Bodhnath. If your time is limited you can take a taxi from Kathmandu via Bodhnath along this same road and return the same way.

## BUDHANILKANTHA

The image of "sleeping Vishnu" at Budhanilkantha is probably the largest reclining image of Vishnu in the world. To get there you can take a bus in the morning from near the National Theatre or alternatively you can travel by bus or tempo to Bansbari, the site of a shoe and leather factory set up with Chinese assistance, and walk in about an hour. The energetic could walk all the way from downtown Kathmandu in a couple of hours or, best of all, ride by bicycle.

Vishnu, sleeping on a bed of snakes, is supposed to have been carved from stone in the 11th century. According to legend Vishnu sleeps continuously for four months of each year, falling asleep with the beginning of the monsoon and awaking when it is over. Each November thousands of pilgrims come here for a big fair on the day he is supposed to wake up. The name Budhanilkantha has nothing to do with Buddha.

Another legend tells of the discovery of the image. A farmer was tilling his field one day and was terrified to find blood coming from the ground at the spot where his plough struck something. An excavation revealed the beautiful image of sleeping Vishnu.

Prayers take place here every morning around 9 am but the kings of Nepal are never allowed to go near the image. Should the king, who is himself supposed to be an incarnation of Vishnu, gaze upon his own image, it is said that he would be cursed. A smaller replica of the image has, therefore, been constructed near the swimming pool at Balaju for the king to visit if he desires. There is also a school, built with British assistance, near Budhanilkantha — it is expected to become the best school in Nepal.

Take a trip to Sheopuri — highest mountain peak of the Valley. It is situated in the northern part and you should first go to Budhanilkantha from where it is a 3 to 4 hour climb — a full day's trip. The scenery is best because of the over 3000m height.

*Wolfgang Korn, West Germany*

## GOKARNA AND SUNDARIJAL

A pleasant couple of hours' walk in the vicinity of the Bodhnath stupa will take you to the old Newar village of Gokarna, north of the Royal Game Reserve. From Bodhnath take the road towards the reserve and turn left on to a dirt road after twenty minutes. Another twenty minutes' walk will bring you to the beautiful three-storied temple of Shiva called Gokarneswar, Lord of Gokarna. The courtyard has an incredible collection of stone statues of deities from Hindu mythology such as Narad, Surya the Sun God, Chandra the Moon God, Kamadeva the God of Love besides the more conventional images of Shiva and Vishnu. Although they are probably only about a century old I have never seen such a collection in one place in Nepal.

After visiting the temple you can walk up to the village which is inhabited entirely by Newars and is surrounded by the game reserve on three sides. Although the village is so close to Kathmandu the villagers are very poor and many do not even speak Nepali. There are deer, monkeys and peacocks in the game reserve. It is a popular picnic spot for Kathmanduites and the entrance fee is only 25 paisa.

Further down the road are the waterfalls of Sundarijal at the edge of the valley; a pleasant bicycle ride down quiet roads.

> The Royal Game Reserve at Gokarna is a nice place to relax and get away from the hassles of Kathmandu.
>
> *Heidi Bauer, USA*

## DAXINKALI

The best-known temple to the Goddess Kali the terrifying is located on the southern edge of the valley. To get there takes about 45 minutes by car passing on the way the narrow Chobar gorge through which flows the Bagmati River. A travel agency tour costs about Rs 50 or you can travel by bus for Rs 5 round trip. The best day to visit Daxinkali is Saturday when crowds of Nepalese journey here to sacrifice chickens and goats to the blood-thirsty goddess. Tuesday is another, quieter, sacrificial day.

The temple is at the bottom of a steep hill with a small stream flowing close by. After their rapid despatch the animals are butchered in the stream and the carcasses will later be brought home for a feast. It is interesting that sacrifices are always made to goddesses and must always be made with young male animals.

> The scene around the altar is one of great chaos, gore and festivity, the visit to Daxinkali recalls the ritual sacrifice of animals which I had only read about in books.
>
> *Jack Peters, USA*

## CHOBAR GORGE

According to legend, when the valley was a lake and Swayambhu an island Manjushree, the God of Wisdom, struck the rock at Chobar with his sword and released the valley's water. With the water thousands of snakes are supposed to have been swept out of the valley — leaving behind the snake king Karkotak who still lives close to the gorge in a pond called Taudaha. The Chobar Gorge is conveniently visited en route to Daxinkali and the beautiful temple of Pharping can also be included on the trip.

Close to the spectacular gorge is the first cement factory in the valley; unfortunately the Kathmandu Valley has a distressing physical similarity to the Los Angeles basin and major industrialisation or a large growth in the number of motor vehicles could lead to a similar affliction — smog.

# Excursions from the Valley

## MOUNTAIN FLIGHT

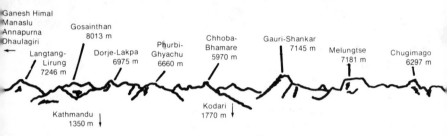

Ganesh Himal
Manaslu
Annapurna
Dhaulagiri

Gosainthan
8013 m

Chhoba-
Bhamare
5970 m

Gauri-Shankar
7145 m

Langtang-
Lirung
7246 m

Dorje-Lakpa
6975 m

Phurbi-
Ghyachu
6660 m

Melungtse
7181 m

Chugimago
6297 m

Kathmandu
1350 m

Kodari
1770 m

If you are in Kathmandu between September and June the mountain flight, with its breathtaking views of the Himalayas, is an experience definitely not to be missed — even at a cost of Rs 375. The flight, made in the early morning, lasts about one hour and the aircraft, a 44-seat pressurised Avro HS 748, flies at an altitude of over 6000 m. During the flight you can view eight of the ten highest mountain peaks in the world from a distance of less than 20 km. The aircraft flies along the length of the mountain range in both directions giving passengers on both sides an equal opportunity to view the peaks. In addition you are allowed to admire the view, individually, from the flight deck. A "mountain profile", to help you identify the peaks, is handed out before departure and after the flight passengers are given a certificate that they have been "greeted" by Mount Everest. The flight is especially exciting during the excellent weather and extremely good visibility of late October and November. Royal Nepal Airlines organise the mountain flights.

## NAGARKOT

The best view of the Himalayas from the vicinity of Kathmandu can be obtained from the village of Nagarkot. Situated on a ridge to the northeast of the valley Nagarkot offers a view stretching from Dhaulagiri in the west to Kanchenjunga in the east.

Several travel agencies offer tours to Nagarkot from Rs 60 but the impecunious can take a bus to Bhaktapur, walk the several km to the ridge

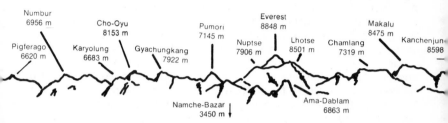

Numbur 6956 m
Cho-Oyu 8153 m
Pumori 7145 m
Everest 8848 m
Makalu 8475 m
Pigferago 6620 m
Karyolung 6683 m
Gyachungkang 7922 m
Nuptse 7906 m
Lhotse 8501 m
Chamlang 7319 m
Kanchenjun 8598
Namche-Bazar 3450 m
Ama-Dablam 6863 m

in a few hours, overnight in Nagarkot and return to Kathmandu for less than Rs 25. During the monsoon period from June to September it is usually cloudy and you will only rarely be rewarded with a glimpse of the mountains. On the other hand the trek to the top will almost always result in a clear view during the months of October to April.

To get to Nagarkot leave the bus stop in Bhaktapur and walk to the centre of town where the Durbar Square is located. Head east from here and ask for the route to Nagarkot. As soon as you leave the city follow the road which passes a Nepalese Army barracks. An hour out from Bhaktapur you reach the city water tank by a cluster of bamboo trees and you can take a shortcut which saves two hours walk. Leave the main motorable road and take the trail to the right. Forty minutes walk brings you to a stream then a steep climb through beautiful pine forests take you back to the main road.

> The road to Nagarkot wanders to the left of the river. A trekker would save time if, after one hour's walk from Bhaktapur, he would follow a pipe that is Bhaktapur's water supply straight to the dam then climb the hill and keep the power line in sight all the way.
>
> *Gary Ott, USA*

Recently a bus service has started from Bhaktapur to the village of Kharepati situated at the foot of the hill where Nagarkot is situated. You can get a bus from the bus station in Bhaktapur as soon as you get off the Kathmandu bus and get to Kharepati for only Rs 1. This service is still irregular. By taking the bus you have to walk only two hours to reach Nagarkot but it is still pleasant to take four hours and walk all the way from Bhaktapur.

There are several lodges at Nagarkot. *Everest Cottage* is about 50m below the ridge and is situated along the road from Bhaktapur, it is run by Indra Bista who used to be a tourist guide in Kathmandu. A double room with attached bathroom costs Rs 20 per bed, Rs 40 if both are occupied. The dining room has a fireplace where guests can enjoy the warmth and eat western food. Near the top of the ridge is the *Everest Lodge* where dormitory beds cost Rs 10. *Nagarkot Guest House* run by a Nepalese woman called Didi has an inn-like atmosphere and charges Rs 5 for a bed in the dormitory and Rs 15 for a single room. A good view of the Himalayan Ranges can be seen from the lodge as it faces the mountains.

If you are overnighting in Nagarkot be certain to bring enough warm clothing as it can get very cold in winter or autumn. There is also camping space 'available. This trip, with its fine views of eight of the ten highest mountain peaks in the world, is one the visitor to Kathmandu should not miss.

## KAKANI

This village is situated on a ridge northwest of Kathmandu and offers good views of the western and central Himalayas. Although I personally prefer the view from Nagarkôt those interested in enjoying the variety of Himalayan scenery, especially magnificent views of Ganesh Himal, should go there. It is quieter than Nagarkot but the food available has less variety and caters less to western tastes. There is a lodge run by the Department of Tourism which charges Rs 10 for a bed or Rs 20 for a single room per night. To get there take a bus or minibus at Sorakhutte to Kaulethan about two hours from Kathmandu on the road to Trisuli. From there it is about one hour's walk along a dirt road to the top of the ridge.

## DHULIKHEL AND NAMOBUDDHA

Dhulikhel, a beautiful village just outside the Kathmandu Valley, gives a better view of the Himalayas than anywhere in the valley. In the late sixties the hippies, who had just started coming to Nepal in large numbers, liked this quiet and sleepy Newar village so much that they decided to construct a temple right on the parade ground where you go to view the mountains.

Although they were not permitted to do so, you may think their choice would not have been a bad one.

> When you are in Dhulikhel, do not miss a visit to Panauti, you reach there after a pleasant two hour walk across ricefields along the course of a small stream. The beauty of this small town is due to its numerous temples and magnificent wood carvings.
>
> *Michel Thierry, France*

Buses leave Kathmandu for Dhulikhel every hour and travel on the excellent road towards the Chinese border. While still in the valley you pass through Thimi, a typical Newar town which produces much of the vegetables for Kathmandu and also has a thriving cottage industry in pottery and mask manufacture. The road then skirts the edge of Bhaktapur and passes through a typical rural landscape of paddy fields at the eastern end of the valley. The road winds over the Sanga Pass as it leaves the valley then descends to Banepa, a Newar town with a population of 10,000 and the biggest bazaar in the area.

A steep climb from Banepa brings you to Dhulikhel at 1500 m. Dhulikhel is the district headquarters and boasts a large number of government offices besides a jail and high school. Its population consists of Newars although there are people of many other castes in surrounding villages. Many tourists make early morning trips to Dhulikhel to see the awesome sunrise over the mountains, travel agencies organise these trips from Rs 80. The budget conscious can travel there by bus and stay overnight for less than Rs 20. The best Himalayan view is obtained by climbing up, in about thirty minutes, the small temple topped hillock to the east.

> To see the sun coming up from behind the mighty Himalayas from the little temple up the hill from Dhulikhel is a thrilling sight, even worth getting up at 4 am.
>
> *Chris Whinett, England*

The *Dhulikhel Lodge* is one of the best cheap places to stay in Nepal. The manager, known as BP to his guests, has visited the US for a few months and is very receptive to western visitors and helpful with trekking information. The spartan rooms at the lodge cost Rs 7.50 per person or Rs 10 in the rooms with the best view. There are also dormitory beds and should the lodge be crowded you may have to be content with these — the lodge is particularly popular with voluntary workers. It is also a good place to meet other travellers.

If possible while in Dhulikhel you should try to make the trek to Namobuddha, also known as Namura. The walk only takes three hours in each direction and is a good practise run for longer treks. This can even be an enjoyable trek during the monsoon season. B.P. will supply you with a diagram showing the trail to Namobuddha, it is not difficult and there are not many steep ascents or descents. From the town you pass to the south of the hill with the temple, although there is a shorter route when returning it is not advisable in the wet season as it may get very slippery.

The trek passes through interesting country and a number of small villages where you can enquire directions. The stupa at Namobuddha is relatively little known and although it is probably not more than a few centuries old I have not been able to discover its exact age. There is an interesting legend behind the stupa at Namobuddha. One of the earlier Buddhas is said to have come across a tiger at the point of death as it was unable to find food for itself or its cubs. The Buddha was so moved by compassion that he offered his own flesh to the hungry tiger. If you climb to the top of the hill from the stupa you reach the site where this event is supposed to have taken place. A carved stone tablet shows Buddha offering his hands to the tiger. You can trek back to Dhulikhel by an alternate route to avoid backtracking.

> You can have some good chang near the Stupa of Namobuddha at a very cheap price.
>
> *Hans Wagner, West Germany*

## THE ROAD TO THE CHINESE BORDER

Only in Hong Kong is it as easy to get so close to China as you can by Nepal's "road to the Chinese border". There is not much to see there but it is nice to boast of having been to the border.

Most of Kathmandu's travel agencies operate tours to the border once or twice a week although it is wise to enquire if the road is blocked by landslides during the monsoon. Kathmandu Travel and Tours (tel 14446) conduct guided tours on Wednesday and Sunday. Everest Travel (tel 12217) has a bus to the border on Sunday, Wednesday and Friday, both agencies charge Rs 120 for the trip which departs at 8 in the morning and returns at 6 in the evening.

Four times daily a public bus service runs between Kathmandu and Barabise via Lamosangu — the starting point for the Everest trek. The first bus leaves at 6 am and the fare is Rs 8. On the way to the border you pass through the beautiful Panchkhal valley between Dhulikhel and

Dolalaghat, a well known area for the production of mangoes, guavas, sugarcane and rice. There are no buses beyond Barabise but you can get a ride on one of the many trucks going to the border for about Rs 5 or you can walk in about five hours. There is a small lodge at Barabise where a single room costs Rs 6. Other ways of getting to the border include a ride in the early morning Post Office bus from Kathmandu or Dhulikhel (which costs Rs 24 round trip) or getting a group together to go on an overland bus or truck.

> You can take the mail car to the border or trek, the scenery as you walk is very nice. It is possible to buy tea in villages on the way and sleep on the floor. The road follows the river and there are many waterfalls. It is reasonably easy to hitchhike along the road (alternatively bargain with lorry drivers) as it is a popular picnic spot.
>
> *Jay McLeary, Australia*

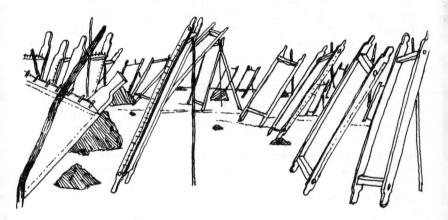

rice paper production

The last stretch to the border is a dirt road running through a spectacular gorge. Shortly after the tarmac road ends there is a site where rice paper is produced. You can see the rice being ground down in a water driven stone mill and the sheets of paper stretched out to dry in the sun. A few km south of the border at Tatopani, hot water in Nepali, there are hot springs if you fancy having a hot bath and watching China at the same time.

At Kodari, a bridge over the river separates Nepal from China. Sentries stand on both ends of the bridge and on the Chinese side there is a small barracks for soldiers. In the late sixties a large portrait of Chairman Mao used to stand near the bridge on the Chinese side but it has since been removed. Nepalese traders and porters are permitted to cross the bridge and go into Tibet as far as the town of Khasa but it is not an open border as is the case with India.

No aspect of Nepalese foreign policy has been watched by the outside world with as much interest, concern and sometimes even alarm as the decisions leading to the construction of this road. Nepal's viewpoint in this respect has not always been understood.

The highway has recently been renamed the Arniko Highway in memory of the renowned Nepalese architect who went to China during the 13th century. The highway starts at Bhaktapur in the Kathmandu Valley; apart from the recently completed trolleybus system between Kathmandu and Bhaktapur the Chinese are also aiding the construction of another road between those two cities. The road leaves the valley through the Sanga Pass and continues through Banepa, Dhulikhel, Panchkhal, Barabise and Tatopani before reaching the Miteri Sanu or "Friendship Bridge" at the Bhote Kosi River. A casual glance at the map will show that at this point a chunk of Chinese territory is almost surrounded by Nepal and this is one of the narrowest points in the whole length of Nepal.

The highway generally follows the alignment of two rivers, an important characteristic of the Chinese constructed highways in Nepal as the Kathmandu to Pokhara road also follows the course of rivers. The length of the highway is 104 km and it includes one major bridge at Dolalghat, by car it takes about four hours to reach the border from Kathmandu. Kodari, the termination point of the highway, is at 1500 m while the Tibetan town of Khasa, across the border, is somewhat higher at an elevation of 2200 m. With the exception of Dhulikhel, few points along the road are noted for their views of the Himalayan range.

The lodge at Tatopani is peaceful and has a lovely setting. The proprietor and his family are hospitable and charming and serve good inexpen-

A    Pharping temple
B    Freak street signs
C    Degutaleju Mandir in Kathmandu

sive food, dinner is just Rs 2. Upstairs where one sleeps there are mats on the floor for Rs 1 or beds for Rs 2. All clean and attractive.

*Sandra Lelaid, Ken Przywaro, USA*

The Chinese road has often been called the best highway in Nepal as there are few hairpin bends or steep sections. There are also comparatively fewer landslides during the monsoons. The bazaar towns along the route, such as Banepa, Dhulikhel and Barabise, are largely Newar but the hinterland is mainly inhabited by Brahmins and Chetris at lower altitudes and by Tamangs and Sherpas at the higher altitudes, particularly in the north.

The agreement for the construction of the road was signed in 1961 and the completed road opened by King Mahendra in 1966. Much of the criticism the road has engendered has been about the threat it could pose to the security of Nepal and India. Nepal has maintained that the road is simply an expansion of a long established trade route and this opening up of a hitherto backward area was essential for Nepal's economic development.

Districts connected by the road have become much closer to Kathmandu and the first third of the road as far as Dhulikhel is heavily trafficked. Even, as far as Dolalghat, the half way point, the volume of traffic makes the road economically feasible. My own conclusions after visiting villages along the road four years after its construction were:

"It could definitely be said that most of the villages in the area are better off today than they were four years ago. It is difficult to reach any conclusion regarding an increase in per capita income or agricultural production but there are now schools in almost every village and villagers now have the opportunity to be at least literate. The opportunity of getting education is not solely restricted to people belonging to higher castes; although caste rules continue to be followed there is a new flexibility in their observation. The number of early marriages has declined greatly but the practise of bigamy is still widespread despite preventive legislation. There is an increased tendency for the educated few of the villages to migrate to Kathmandu and settle there. Almost every village has a transistor radio and the villagers now have a chance to know what is happening in Nepal as well as in foreign countries."

A    Mani stones in the Solu Khumbu
B    Machhapuchhare from Bindebasini temple in Pokhara
C    Chorten and mani wall in the Solu Khumbu

One of the largest magnesite deposits in Asia has been discovered a few km east of the road. If it were not for the road this deposit would never have been economically feasible. A road from Lamosangu to Jiri, to be built with a Swiss loan, is envisaged to pass through this deposit. The road has also made substantial indirect contributions to Nepal's economic development. Half the materials and machinery used in the construction of other Chinese-aided projects in Nepal, such as the Sun Khosi hydroelectric project producing 10,000 kw near Lamosangu or the Kathmandu-Pokhara highway, are estimated to have been brought along the road. Nevertheless the bordering region in Tibet is sparsely populated and economic activity is still low. It is also a long way from the populated and industrialised areas of China. It is often cheaper to import materials from China by the sea route via Calcutta than directly along the road but this will change as soon as there is more economic activity in the area.

## TIGER TOPS

The Tiger Tops jungle camp is located in the Chitwan Valley 130km southwest of Kathmandu. The office of Tiger Tops (tel 12706) is located on Durbar Marg close to the Hotel de L'Annapurna. Tiger Tops operate a tent camp on the banks of the Narayani River in the National Park and also a more comfortable and expensive, *Jungle Lodge*. A return flight to Meghauly, close to the camp and lodge costs $US46. Accommodation per night in the tent camp costs $US29 including meals, tours and park camping fee. In addition there is a Rs 20 entry fee to the park. In the *Jungle Lodge* first night cost is $US70 in a single room, $US129 in a double room, this reduces to $US45/$US85 by the third night. Accommodation costs include transportation from the airstrip in both cases — you travel by elephant if going to the *Jungle Lodge.* Dr Charles McDougal, who holds a doctorate in anthropology and is an authority on the people and wildlife of Nepal, gives lectures on the area and the animals in the park.

> **Tiger Tops Lodge** — Tiger Tops, PO Box 242, Kathmandu — Telex NP 216 TIGTOP — Kathmandu office tel 12706 — 20 rooms all with bath — restaurant — bar

In the park there is opportunity for boating and canoeing, visits to native villages, fishing for mahseer in season, nature walks and treks, elephant treks, swimming and, of course, wildlife observation. Unlike African animals, which tend to move in large herds, Asian wildlife is more solitary and shy. Seeing wildlife can be a case of patience and searching but animals you may see include a variety of deer, sloth bear, wild boar, fresh water dolphins, crocodiles (careful where you swim!), the rare Great Indian one-horned rhinoceros, leopard and, with a good deal of luck, the very rare and elusive Royal Bengal tiger. Best season for visiting the park is from October to March when the weather is not too hot. Hunting is strictly prohibited. It is estimated that there are 300 rhinos and 30 tigers in the park which is only a third of the number 25 years ago. Tiger Tops can also be reached after a two day raft trip on the Trisuli and Narayani Rivers. The trip starts at Mugling on the Kathmandu-Pokhara Highway and reaches Tiger Tops the next day after camping by the side of the river.

There are two possibilities for visiting the Park less expensively. *Gaida Wildlife Camp* is located in Sauraha near Tadi Bazar in the Chitwan National Park. Guests stay in cabins for $US110 for the first three days which covers the cost of meals, air fares to and from Kathmandu and elephant rides. Their office in Kathmandu is at Durbar Marg (tel 13976). *Elephant Camp* which is located in the same area has well equipped huts by the side of the Rapti River. You can either fly to Bharatpur and be taken to the camp by a vehicle or take a bus to Hetauda and then to Tadi, which will be cheaper. The airfare to and from Bharatpur is $US20. It costs about $US90 for the first three days including transport, board, lodging and elephant rides. It is considerably cheaper if you go there by yourself and find a room. The park can also be visited on the cheap:

To get to the elephant camp take the east-west highway from Hetauda on the Kathmandu-Birganj road.Tadi Bazar is about four hours by bus or truck from Hetauda and from there it is an hour and a half by foot to the camp. The path leads south from the town centre or from the track heading south just after crossing the small bridge at the west end of the bazar.

While the normal procedure is to first get a permit from the Wildlife Department or Tiger Tops, persons arriving without permits are usually accommodated. A National Park entrance fee of Rs 20 is valid for entries for a week. To avoid the daily Rs 10 camping fee for sleeping within the park boundaries, nearby tea houses and *bhattis* can provide space for your sleeping bag. Renting elephants for a day costs Rs 105 and provides seats for two or three passengers to take you off across the Rapti River and into the jungle to see, often at extremely close range, the huge rhinos. The ride lasts for several hours if you wish, when taking a first ride early in the day a second may be possible in the afternoon. While I've had good luck in viewing rhinos in the October and April seasons, the recommended best time for observing them is in the March to May dry season when the five to ten m high elephant grass is gone.

I cannot commend enough this exciting and spectacular opportunity — for a few dollars one of the finest wildlife experiences in Asia is available to the low budget traveller in Nepal.

*Rob Burati, USA*

# Pokhara

If the work of man has impressed you in the Kathmandu Valley it will be the work of nature which will cast a lasting spell on your visit to Pokhara. The skyline is dominated by the Annapurna range and the perfectly shaped peak of Macchapuchhare, the fish-tail mountain. The Himalayas seem much closer than they do in Kathmandu. A member of a mountaineering expedition, speaking of the view from Pokhara, said:

> Compared to that vision, the Matterhorn would have looked crude, the peerless Weisshorn a flattened hump.

Toni Hagen, the Swiss geologist who, in the late fifties, was the first foreigner to travel extensively in Nepal, described the view from Pokhara:

> Nepal is a land of contrast. Nowhere is this more clearly seen than here in Pokhara ... in the background, with no intermediate range between, the Annapurna chain rises abruptly to an altitude of over 8000 metres.

The Pokhara Valley contains three lakes, Phewatal, the most beautiful and accessible, is only about fifteen minutes walk from the airport; the others are Rupa and Begnas lakes. The hills around Pokhara are inhabited largely by 'Gurungs — a tribal people who form one of the important constituents of the Gurkha Rifles in both the Indian and British armies. Picturesque Gurung villages like Ghandruk and Siklis are within a few walking days of Pokhara and are really worth the effort to visit. The population of the valley itself consists largely of Brahmins and Chetris. The long tradition of providing Gurkha soldiers from this area means that Pokhara has long been open to outside influence but there is still much population pressure from the surrounding hills. The salaries and pensions brought from employment outside in the army or Indian households helps to improve conditions in this food deficient area.

The area around Pokhara is currently changing very rapidly. The construction of the road linking Pokhara to the Indian border and to Kathmandu, previously it was accessible only by flying or walking, had a major impact on the area. Pokhara is also the growth centre for mid-western Nepal in the country's four region development programme.

Pokhara is about 700 m lower than Kathmandu and as a result rather warmer and more pleasant in late autumn and winter. On the other hand it is not a good place to visit in the monsoon as Pokhara gets twice the rainfall of Kathmandu.

## GETTING TO POKHARA

There are bus and minibus services between Kathmandu and Pokhara and from there to the Indian border. Public buses from Kathmandu can be found at the foot of the Bhimsen Tower near the Post Office or at the bus stand near the City Hall. The buses leave in the early morning and it is advisable to reserve tickets at least a day in advance, cost is only Rs 22. These are the same kind of public buses that make the trip up from the Indian border — they are not very comfortable and you may have difficulty in stretching your legs.

More comfortable, although slightly more expensive, are the minibuses which are usually ex-overland vehicles. On these buses the cost is Rs 30 to 35 and tickets are sold from offices around Freak Street or in hotels. An advantage to travelling by minibus is that they will take you to the lake area of Pokhara. The public buses only go as far as the airport/bus stand from where it is expensive to get a taxi to the lake or entails a half hour walk. The buses will also pick you up from the lake area for the return trip. It takes five or six hours to travel between the two towns.

There are frequent flights between Kathmandu and Pokhara, the short flight offers good Himalayan views and costs Rs 150. If you decide to travel by road there are few dangerous curves or steep ascents and descents along the excellent Kathmandu-Pokhara highway.

## KATHMANDU-POKHARA HIGHWAY

The Kathmandu-Pokhara highway is 202 km long and for the most part follows the courses of three major rivers — the Trisuli, Marsyangdi and the Seti and crosses over two rivers — the Madi and Marsyangdi. The portion from Naubise, where the road to the Indian border splits off, is 176 km long and was constructed with Chinese assistance — when completed in the early seventies it had cost approximately $14 million.

From the fertile valley of Naubise the road follows the small stream of Mahesh Khola for twenty-two km to its junction with the Trisuli River at Galchi Bazar. The road then follows the Trisuli river through Gajuritar and Benighat, where the big Budhi Gandaki River joins the Trisuli from the north, to the confluence of the Marsyangdi and Trisuli at Mugling. This is the halfway point and a popular lunch stop; at an altitude of only 280 m it is also the lowest point along the highway. The Chinese have also planned a road leading south from Mugling to the Chitwan Valley where Tiger Tops is located. The sacred Hindu temple of Mankamana is only a few km away on the top of a steep hill.

One of the longest suspension bridges in Nepal crosses the Trisuli from Mugling and follows the course of the Marsyangdi. The combination of these two rivers is known as the Gandak, one of the major tributaries of the Ganges. About an hour from Mugling the road passes Dumre, a new town settled after the construction of the highway, just above it on a hilltop is the beautiful town of Bandipur. The capital of the principality of Gorkha, from where the unification of Nepal started, is northeast of this area in the hills. The road then continues through Damauli, district headquarters and a good sized bazaar, across the Madi River by a big bridge and on to Khaireni, headquarters of an agricultural extension project being implemented with assistance from West Germany. Improved seed and fertilizers are being provided to many villages in the area from this project; the project buildings are visible from the bus. From here the road follows the River Seti through Sisuwa only twelve km from Pokhara and near the two smaller lakes of the valley. The road enters the town about halfway between the airport and the bazaar. At some points along the route, especially between Mugling and Pokhara, you can glimpse Himalchuli, Manaslu, the Annapurnas and other peaks during the autumn and winter.

> Damoli, a small town on the road between Kathmandu and Pokhara, is worth a stopover. The town's main road leads to the Panchayat building. Taking the path to the left of it will take you down to the Madi and Seti Rivers for bathing — go upstream a hundred or so yards on the right to reach a beach.
>
> *Mike Baldwin, USA*

> The land one sees along the route from Kathmandu to Pokhara is like a patchwork quilt — a composite of swathes of beauty from round the world. I saw rock gorge river scenes from Japanese brush paintings, hills akin to the south-west of the US as well as those from the highlands of Scotland, and the gracefully sculptured terraces, cousins to Java and Bali — consecutive changes in a day's drive.
>
> *Judy Benewitz, USA*

## ORIENTATION IN POKHARA

By air or bus your arrival will be at the airport which also serves as the bus stand. The main market or bazaar is located to the north of the bus stand while the lake area, where most visitors stay, is south. It is a long walk from the bus stop and taxis are reluctant to drive to the lake for less than Rs 10. On the other hand small taxis and minibuses shuttle between the bazaar and airport. The standard rate is Rs 1 by taxi, only 50 paisa by bus, from the airport to Mahendra Pool, located at the newer part at the beginning of the bazaar. The fare from the airport to Bagar at the far end of the bazaar is Rs 2. There are usually no buses after 5pm.

**Bazaar area:** Pokhara Bazaar consists of a two km long street, poorly planned and poorly laid out entailing long walks to get from place to place. Most of the modern shops and the Post Office are located around Mahendra Pool, there are very few shops in the lake area. If you continue along the bazaar from Mahendra Pool and then turn left you reach Pokhara's only cinema, a further twenty minutes walk will take you to the quite modern Shining Mission Hospital which is run by wester

# The Himalayas

## THE MOUNTAINS

The mountains — main peaks from east to west:

| Peak | Height | First Ascent | |
|------|--------|--------------|---|
| Kanchenjunga | 8598 m | 1955 British | |
| Makalu | 8475 m | 1955 French | |
| Lhotse | 8501 m | 1955 Swiss | |
| Everest | 8848 m | 1953 British | |
| Nuptse | 7906 m | 1961 British | |
| Cho Oyu | 8153 m | 1954 Austrian | |
| Gauri Shankar | 7145 m | — | |
| Phurbi Ghyachu | 5722 m | — | ⬆ |
| Dorje Lakpa | 6975 m | — | visible from Kathmandu |
| Langtang | 7246 m | 1959 Japanese | |
| Ganesh Himal | 7406 m | 1955 Franco-Swiss | ⬇ |
| Himalchuli | 7892 m | 1960 Japanese | |
| Manaslu | 7850 m | 1956 Japanese | |
| Annapurna | 8090 m | 1950 French | |
| Annapurna 2 | 7937 m | 1960 British, Indo-Nepal | ⬆ |
| Annapurna 3 | 7502 m | 1961 Indian | visible from Pokhara |
| Annapurna 4 | 7525 m | 1955 German | |
| Macchapuchhare | 7059 m | — | |
| Dhaulagiri | 8137 m | 1960 Swiss | ⬇ |

Nepal has the highest peak in the world — Mt Everest — and six others over 8000 m and it was mountain climbers attempting to conquer the "top of the world" who were amongst the first "tourists" to enter Nepal. Most of the major peaks were climbed in the fifties and sixties but Himalayan mountaineering has lost none of its appeal.

While trekking you are unlikely to go above 3500 m unless you are walking to the Everest base camp but breathtaking views are easily found. Mt Everest is not visible from the Kathmandu Valley but from Nagarkot on top of the ridge to the eastern end of the valley you can pick it out in the distance. The view here extends from the extreme east of Nepal to Dhaulagiri in the west. Dhulikhel also provides a fine Himalayan panorama although Everest is not so clearly visible. Kakani, to the northwest of Kathmandu, provides a good view of the western Himalayas, particularly Ganesh Himal. A very fine view can be had from Daman on the road to the

Indian border — a mountain profile to help you identify the peaks from Nagarkot or Daman can be obtained from the tourist information office. If your stay in Kathmandu permits, a visit to Sheopuri to the north and Phulchoki to the south is also worthwhile.

A number of peaks are clearly visible from Kathmandu particularly Ganesh Himal, its three peaks are seen slightly to the northwest. The lesser peaks of Dorje Lakpa (6799 m) and Chobha Bhamare (5970 m) almost dominate the Kathmandu skyline. East of Ganesh Himal the snow-covered peak of Langtang can be seen partially hidden by closer mountains. East of Dorje Lakpa the massive block descending slowly to the east is Phurbi Ghyachu. Further to the east no major peaks are visible until the massive bulk of Gauri Shankar, which can only be seen from the northeast of the valley.

The view from Pokhara is much better than from Kathmandu and a walk up to Sarangkot is worthwhile for the startling span of the Annapurnas with the perfectly symetrical shape of Machhapuchhare standing before them. If you are trekking northwest a trip to Pun Hill just above Ghodepani will provide an incredible sight. Machhapuchhare gets its unusual name, the "fish tail" mountain from its split appearance when viewed from the east — it is still a "virgin", unclimbed, peak. In Nepali Annapurna means "full of grain" and this long series of ridges do indeed look like the result of a recent harvest.

> On the Jomosom trek the view from Pun Hill (near Ghodepani) on a clear morning is the most beautiful sight I have seen anywhere in the world. If it is cloudy at Ghodepani it is worth waiting for as long as it takes to clear.
>
> *R. McArthur, England*

## MOUNTAINEERING

The sport of mountaineering came into vogue in Europe during the Victorian era and once the major Alpine peaks had been conquered European mountaineers naturally turned their eyes to the greater challenge of the Himalayas. The natural difficulties in climbing these far higher mountains were compounded during the twenties and thirties by the continued seclusion of Nepal. Expeditions were chiefly launched from the Tibetan side of the range and, attempting the major prize first, were mainly on Mt Everest.

In 1921, 1922 and 1924 a series of British attempts on the world's highest peak resulted in a maximum height of 8572 m, just 300 m short of the summit. This height was actually reached, in 1924, without the use of oxygen although the earlier 1922 expedition had used it to reach 8326 m. Already by this time the pattern for future expeditions with their large contingent of porters had been set — the 1924 expedition used 350.

In 1925 the British climbers Mallory, who coined the famous mountaineer's explanation "because it's there", and Irvine disappeared in an attempt that may have actually reached the summit — their bodies were never found. A series of less successful attempts followed through the 1930s although several did succeed in climbing to beyond 8000 m. A strange solo attempt in 1934 by Maurice Wilson added another name to those climbers who lost their lives on Everest.

After the war greater affluence in the west, improved equipment, skills and oxygen apparatus together with the reopening of Nepal led to a series of new assaults both on Everest and other peaks. In 1951 a reconnaissance expedition included amongst its numbers the New Zealand climber Edmund Hillary, and a Swiss expedition in 1952 sent Sherpa climber Norkay Tensing to 7500 m. Finally in 1953 John Hunt's British team succeeded in getting Tensing and Hillary to the highest spot on earth.

Once conquered, success on Everest followed repeatedly, a Swiss expedition reached the top in 1956 and in 1960 it was the turn of a party from the People's Republic of China. Members of the massive American expedition on 1963, nearly 1000 climbers and porters, found the Chinese flag on top. An Indian expedition reached the summit in 1965 and in 1970 a Japanese team not only reached the top but sent one fearless climber back down on skis! Several more attempts included a successful Italian team in 1973 and the International Women's Year victory of the Japanese women's party.

Other Himalayan peaks had also been comprehensively attacked in the fifties and sixties. The successful French expedition under Maurice Herzog on Annapurna in 1950 was probably the best known for not only was this the first peak over 8000 m to "fall" but the mountain fought back, forcing the climbers to descend from the summit in appalling weather. Badly frostbitten, Herzog and his partner paid dearly for their challenge in fingers and toes. While the large expeditions successfully reached the top of one major peak after another, a new breed of up and coming climbers were cutting their teeth on Alpine and North American peaks. Eschewing the "easy" routes they went for the most difficult faces, attacking them with carefully developed skills and high technology space age equipment. Chris Bonnington exemplified this trend with his 1970 climb on the south face of Annapurna and followed this up with a skillfully orchestrated rush to the top of Everest by the "impossible" southwest face in 1975.

Mountain climbing is now looked upon by the government of Nepal as a useful source of income as well as a generator of publicity. A royalty has to be paid for each attempt — the higher the peak the greater the fee. Detailed applications have to be made and at present Everest is fully booked for years to come! Only one expedition is allowed on any given peak in each season — the post-monsoon and pre-monsoon parts of the dry season. For a time in the 1960s the government actually stopped all expeditions.

There are still many major peaks which have not been successfully climbed, some not even attempted but some observers hope the next wave of activity may be a retreat from the massive, costly, high technology expeditions to a smaller more manageable scale. Kathmandu's trekking shops have so much high quality equipment gleaned from the left overs of major expeditions that a small party could be equipped right there.

ROYAL NEPAL AIRLINES

yeti
SERVICE

### The Yeti

No description of Nepal can be complete without a mention of the famous yeti — the abominable snowman. This mysterious, ape-like creature lives high in the remotest regions of the Himalayas and has been talked and written about, feared by hill people, searched for by westerners, "seen" by countless people — but never photographed. Footprints in the snow are the only trace the shy yeti likes to leave but these are often thought to be normal size human prints that have grown as the sun melted the snow around them. Similarly the yeti scalps in the Solu Khumbu region, in particular the one at the Pangboche monastery, have all turned out to be fake. Despite the scientific reluctance to accept the yeti's existence everyone would like to believe in it — so keep your camera handy when trekking!

# Trekking

Trekking — hiking along the trails that form the main links between Nepal's isolated villages and settlements — is one of the country's main attractions. The word "trekking" was almost unheard of in Nepal until the last decade but many of today's visitors come to Nepal solely to trek.

## WHY TREK

A trek in Nepal is a unique and unforgettable experience for a whole range of reasons but four in particular stand out:

**Scenery:** Eight of the ten highest mountains in the world are in Nepal and if you want to see them from close up you must walk. While trekking you'll see far more than mountains — you can walk from tropical lowlands to alpine meadows and glacial moraines while in the spring Nepal's brilliant rhododendrons will be in bloom and you may see rare species of Himalayan birds.

**Safety:** Not only is the scenery interesting and ever changing but it can be seen in safety. Theft, robbery, assault — all the problems of western civilisations and many Asian countries — are unknown in Nepal. Women can safely trek alone in Nepal as did a young woman from Metz in France whom I met recently — not only did she trek alone but she did not speak English or Nepali!

**Diversity:** Nepal is a country of contrasts and this extends to the people as well as the landscape. Trekkers pass through picturesque villages inhabited by Sherpas, Gurungs, Magars, Newars, Brahmins, Tamangs and the many other ethnic groups which co-exist in Nepal.

**People:** Trekkers are always impressed by the friendliness of the people they meet along the local trails which are in constant use and humming with activity. This is a totally different experience from hiking along the often uninhabited trails in the US Rockies, European Alps or Australian bushland. Above all no household in a village would turn away a weary traveller arriving late in the evening — there are frequent possibilities of staying in Nepali homes.

## ON THE TRAIL

A trek can last half a day or for over a month. A short walk up to Nagarkot to see the sunrise only takes about three hours while the walk to the Everest Base Camp will take at least three weeks. Make sure you enjoy walking before setting out on a long trek!

## POPULAR TREKS

| Trek | Location | Time | From — To |
|------|----------|------|-----------|
| Everest | to Solu Khumbu region of east Nepal | 1 to 5 weeks | Bus to Lamosangu or fly to Lukla then walk to the base camp |
| Langtang | North of Kathmandu | 12 days | Bus to Trisuli then walk to the Langtang Valley |
| Helambu | North of Kathmandu | 7 days | Bus to Panchka or go via Sundarijal |
| Kathmandu-Sheopuri | Highest point on the hill north of Kathmandu | 8 hours | Walk from Budhanilkantha and return via Sundarijal |
| Kathmandu-Nagarkot | Hilltop north-east of Kathmandu | 3 hours up | Bus to Bhaktapur then walk |
| Dhulikhel-Namobuddha | East of Kathmandu Valley | One day | Bus to Dhulikhel then walk |
| Annapurna Sanctuary | North of Pokhara | 12 days | Walk from Pokhara via Naudanda, Birethanti and Ghandruk |
| Ghandruk-Ghodepani | North of Pokhara | 7 days | Walk from Pokhara to Ghandruk |
| Pokhara-Jomosom-Muktinah | North-west of Pokhara | 12 days | Routes via Birethanti or via Kusma and Beni |
| Manang | North-east of Pokhara | 2 weeks | Dumre to Manang |
| Pokhara-Sarangkot | North of Pokhara | One day | Walk from Bindebasini temple in Pokhara bazar |

| Maximum Height | Interesting Sights | Comments |
|---|---|---|
| Tyangboche — 3875 m<br>Kala Patar — 5545 m | Walk through interesting Sherpa villages to stunning views of Everest, Ama Dablam, Nuptse, Lhotse | very touristy from Lukla on |
| 4200 m | Pass through ethnically Tibetan villages like Tamang, en route to the glacier at the foot of Langtang peak | stay in lodges along trail |
| Tarkeghyang —<br>2800 m | Friendly people and chances to stay in Sherpa homes but poor views of the peaks | — |
| 2700 m | Walk through forests with excellent mountain views, can overnight in a tent | — |
| 2000 m | Good scenery including Everest, can overnight in a lodge | — |
| 1700 m | Pleasant one-day walk along a typical trail to an old stupa marking a legendary spot | — |
| 3725 m | Pass through Gurung villages en route to the foot of Annapurna, excellent views | 2 days through uninhabited areas |
| 2700 m | Excellent views of Annapurna and Machhapuchhare en route to village of Ghandruk | Need guide from Ghandruk to Ghodepani |
| 2700 m | Most interesting trek in Nepal, cross the Himalayan range between Annapurna and Dhaulagiri | — |
| 3600 m | Valley north of Annapurna Range inhabited by Tibetan speaking people known as Manangis | Only open since 1976, can reach Muktinah by 5600 m pass |
| 1700 m | Excellent views of Annapurna and the Pokhara Valley, see ruins of a 17th century fort | — |

**Height:** Trekking is not mountaineering but it is as well to remember that the Himalayas begin where other mountains finish. An average trek oscillates between 1000 m and 3000 m but the trek to the Everest base camp will reach 5545 m. Most of the time you will remain within the altitude range 1500 m to 2000 m. It is important to remember that 4000 m in Nepal is not the same as in Europe or North America as the country is much closer to the equator.

**A Day on the Trail:** Trekking usually consists of a series of ascents or descents, walking five or six hours in the day. To ensure good acclimatisation at high altitudes it is wise to halt for the night at a lower level than the high point reached during the day. A long midday meal stop is usually made and night will be spent in a village tea shop or in camp — depending whether the trekker is by himself or with an organised trekking company.

**When to Trek:** The best trekking season is in October and November just after the monsoon —visibility will be clear and the weather mild. March is the next best season and has the added bonus of the rhododendrons and other flowers. Trekking can be done and enjoyed in December, January and February but it can get very cold — particularly at night. April and May are good months for doing high altitude trekking but trekking is not possible between June and September when the monsoon rains make the trails extremely slippery and the leeches come out to make walking miserable. Some people do trek in early June and late September.

**Where to Stay?** If you are trekking independently you stay either in tea houses or in private homes in villages. If you are with an organised trekking group everything is taken care of and you will sleep mainly in tents set up by the porters. Some tea stalls and homes have started making a small charge, Rs 1 to 5, for an overnight stay but usually accommodation is free providing you take the evening meal there. If you go by yourself to an uninhabited area you may have to sleep in a cave or an abandoned inn.

## PRELIMINARIES

**Trekking Permits:** Every trekker must carry a trekking permit when away from the areas permitted in the visa. No trekking permits are however, needed for walking in the Kathmandu or Pokhara Valley or along short treks such as Dhulikhel and Namobuddha. Trekking permits are issued for one destination at a time along prescribed routes. Trekking permits cost Rs 15 initially and an extra Rs 15 for each week's trek. The trekking permit can only be obtained and extended in Kathmandu.

**Equipment:** If you do not already have good equipment it can be bought or rented from one of the trekking shops. The equipment is often top quality but although daily rental charges are reasonable a large deposit may be required — a good down-filled sleeping bag, a rucksack, down pants and down jackets can each be rented for around Rs 5 per day but the total deposit can easily come to over $US100. It is advisable to have your own strong, comfortable boots — they can be rented but people with large feet may have trouble finding suitable footwear. If a rented sleeping bag does not look perfectly clean have it dry cleaned. *Himal Hiking Home* in Yetkha, one block from Durbar Square, and *Annapurna Mountaineering and Trekking* in Thamel have a wide range of gear, you can find some items in Freak Street. Trekking equipment can also be rented in Pokhara. Try *Pokhara Pony Treks* whose office is located along the route from the airport to the lake.

**Incidentals:** The food available along the trail is normally limited in its variety so bring along some cheese, dried fruit and canned food. It will be almost impossible to change money along the way so bring adequate Nepali currency in small denominations. Take cigarettes and matches, they're widely appreciated small gifts. Please don't spoil the children who in some regions come up asking for "one rupee". A torch is indispensable for late night trips to the outhouse and matches or salt for getting rid of leeches if you trek in the wet.

**Health:** Medical care along the trail is almost non-existent except for the Edmund Hillary hospital at Khumjung in the Solu Khumbu so make sure you are fit and healthy before departing. A rescue helicopter is extremely expensive! Take care of yourself along the trail by ensuring that water is boiled — remember that fresh tea is always safe. Diarrhoea can be the curse of trekkers so bring appropriate medication. At high altitudes almost everyone suffers from headaches so aspirin are advisable as are sleeping tablets to ensure a good sleep. Sunburn can also be a problem at altitude, a barrier cream will protect your skin and good sunglasses are necessary for your eyes. Blisters are another problem for the trekker and adequate supplies of band aids and moleskin are advisable. The most serious health problem the unwary trekker can fall prey to is the dreaded mountain sickness — this is a serious, even deadly, danger for the careless or foolhardy trekker. Mountain sickness is a form of pulmonary oedema and usually hits young and healthy people who do not heed the warnings and go "too high, too fast". Prevention is simple — take things easy and ensure plenty of acclimatisation, the symptoms often first show themselves at night and this is why it is best to sleep at a lower altitude than the maximum reached during the day. The mild symptoms are low urine output, bad headaches, sleeplessness and loss of appetite, followed in severe cases by nausea, vomiting, severe fatigue, mental confusion, breathlessness and apathy. If you get mountain sickness there's just one answer — get down to a lower altitude as quickly and with as little effort as possible.

**Maps:** The series of *Mandala* trekking maps are readily available in shops in Kathmandu. They include Kathmandu to Pokhara, Pokhara to Jomosom, Jomosom to Jumla and Surkhet, Lamosangu to Mt Everest, and Helambu-Langtang. They include a useful glossary of Nepali words and walking times along the trails.

hill country ambulance service

## ARRANGEMENTS

**Independent Trekking:** Most of the young people visiting Nepal trek independently. While the organized treks have all arrangements made by the trekking agencies, including porters and food, the independent traveller carries his own luggage (or just hires a porter), spends overnight at tea stalls, lodges, and sometimes private homes along the way and eats local food. Although little English is spoken in the villages along most of the trekking routes, it is becoming more easily understood. *Sherpa Trekking Services*, Kamaladi, (Tel 12489) have specialized in low cost trekking and will still be able to help you organize a trek at minimum cost. They can also arrange the services of a porter or English speaking guides or rent trekking equipment — except during the peak trekking season (October — November and March — April).

Independent trekking is much easier with the services of a porter who can be hired for Rs 18 to Rs 30 per day. This aid to easy trekking is particularly invaluable at high altitudes where just getting up the ascents will be quite sufficient effort for most people. When agreeing a price with a porter make sure whether or not you are paying for the porter's meals. In the hills porters can easily be found at most villages or at the airfields where there will usually be porters who have just despatched a group back to Kathmandu. Porters do not usually speak English but will help you find overnight accommodation as well as carry the load and act as a guide.

**Organised Trekking:** Several trekking companies in Nepal will arrange sleeping bags, porters, tents, food and provide experienced English-speaking Sherpa guides. All you need to carry is your own clothes and camera. Trek charges vary from $US17 to $US30 per day depending upon the number of people in the group and the duration of the trek. Probably the best known trekking organisation in Nepal is *Mountain Travel* (tel 12808; PO Box 170) whose well-known manager Col J. O. M. Roberts has organised many mountaineering expeditions. Their American office is Mountain Travel, 1398 Folano Ave, Albany, California 94706, and in England their treks can be booked through Thomas Cook, 45 Berkeley St, London. Their treks cost between $US30 and $US40 per day.

*Annapurna Mountaineering and Trekking* on Durbar Marg (tel 12736, PO Box 795) is also well known and charges between $US20 and $US24 per day. *Trans Himalayan Trekking*, also on Durbar Marg (tel 13854, P.O. Box 989), can be booked through Trail Finders in Australia or England or by Treasure Tours in New Zealand. Their American manager has written a book on trekking published by Lonely Planet Publications.

*Ausventure* are a very well known and respected name for organising treks from Australia. Their address is PO Box 54, Moxman, NSW 2088.

Many British trekkers organise their treks through *Sherpa Expeditions*, 3 Bedford Rd, London W4.

*Himalayan Trekking* on Ramshah Path (tel 11808, PO Box 391) charge $US18 to $US25 per day and have a Sherpa who has conquered Everest. *Sherpa Trekking*, Kamaladi (tel 12489, PO Box 500) is the least expensive trekking company at $US17 to $US24 per day, they also give student concessions. Other trekking agencies in Nepal include: *Sherpa Co-Operative Trekking*, PO Box 1339, Kamal Pokhari (tel 15887); *Himalayan Rover Trek*, PO Box 1081, Ramshah Path (tel 12691); and *Himalayan Shangrila Trek*, Ramshah Path (tel 13303).

All the organised trekking companies require plenty of notice to fix a trek, try to allow at least two months.

## TREKS

There are countless different routes and treks around Nepal, the following are just a few of the most popular "standard" routes.

## EVEREST TREK

The trek to the base camp at the foot of Mt Everest takes three weeks at a minimum. This trek is not as easy as trekking in the Pokhara area as the trail traverses regions which have remained relatively backward and closed to outside influences. The Sherpa country in the vicinity of Everest is an exception of course since there have been so many mountaineering expeditions in this area in the past twenty-five years.

The usual starting point for the trek is Lamosangu on the road to the Chinese border but if time is short the trek can be shortened by flying between Kathmandu and Lukla, only a few days walk from the base camp. If you only intend to fly one way it is best to fly back from Lukla as this gives greater acclimatisation to the altitude. If you fly direct from Kathmandu at 1300 m to Lukla at 2800 m and then start climbing to the base camp at 5340 m great care must be taken that you gain sufficient acclimatisation. Flights to Lukla are now on a regular basis but at the height of the trekking season, although departures are frequent, cloudy weather can easily shut the hill country STOL fields for several days at a time. Per person cost is about $US40.

The Everest trek is relatively rough as you have many ascents and descents to make. Between Lamosangu and Surkya near Lukla the trail repeatedly climbs over mountain passes as high as 3500 m and then descends to valleys as low as 1000 m while crossing the rivers that run from the north. There are occasional bazaars and market places along the way. From Surkya at 2343 m to Namche Bazar, 3440 m, and on to the base camp at 5340 m is almost continuously up. It has been estimated that a trekker from Lamosangu to the base camp makes total ascents and descents approaching twice the height of Everest!

On the way you pass through villages inhabited by Tamangs, Sunuwars, Rais and finally Sherpas plus some Brahmin-Chetri villages and occasional Newari ones, mainly the bazaars. In other words you walk from the Nepali speaking, Hindu lowlands to the mongoloid, Tibetan-Buddhist highlands with many opportunities to observe Nepal's rich ethnic mixture. The most interesting area to visit in the Everest trek is the Sherpa country situated at the foot of Everest. You are actually in Sherpa country after you reach Changma or Junibesi while walking from Lamosangu or in Lukla if you fly from Kathmandu. According to the findings of a well known British anthropologist, no other Tibetan speaking people in Nepal could be compared to the Sherpas "in the high standard of living, spirit of enterprise, sense of civic responsibility, social polish and general devotion to the practice of Buddhism".

The main crop of the Khumbu area is potato. Although the economy of Sherpa villages depended on potato cultivation, itself a recent introduction, tourism is becoming increasingly important. New Zealand is helping Nepal in setting up the Everest National Park. The park will be located in the catchment area of the Dudhkosi and Imja Rivers. Under the project, attempts will be made to conserve forest, landscape and wildlife in the area, provide facilities for visitors and raise the standard of living of the local people.

### Day 1: Kathmandu-Lamosangu-Perko (3 hours walking)

Buses leave Kathmandu at 6 am, 10 am and 2 pm on the three to four hour trip to Lamosangu. In Nepali Lamosangu means "long bridge", the town is situated on the banks of the Sunkosi River and is the site for a Chinese-aided 10,000 Kw hydroelectric power plant.

The first part of the trek involves a steep eight-hour ascent from Lamosangu at 770 m to Muldi at 2345 m but you can stop at Perko (1661 m) three hours from Lamosangu.

### Day 2: Perko-Shera (8 hours walking)

From Perko you continue to ascend for five hours to Muldi then commence to descend to Surke (1750 m) and finally Shera at 1448 m.

### Day 3: Shera-Yarsa (8 hours walking)

For a short distance from Shera you walk through pine forests before reaching Kiratichap (1320 m) then descend to the Bhote Kosi River and climb over 1000 m to the Yarsa at 1974 m.

### Day 4: Yarsa-Jiri (5 hours walking)

A 500 m climb brings you to the Chisapani Pass from where you have a good view of the eastern Himalayas and in particular Gauri Shankar which lies immediately to the north. An overnight stay in the beautiful 1860 m valley of Jiri is worthwhile, the valley was developed with Swiss assistance in the sixties and has a STOL field and hospital. The guest house here costs only Rs 2 per day and has private rooms and running water, very pleasant after three days walking. The weekly market, or *hat*, is held on Saturdays and is well worth seeing.

> On the Everest trek it is a good idea to rest for a day or two at the Government Agricultural Centre at Jiri which is about three days trek from Lamosangu. Tourists can stay in modern stone bungalows (two beds to each room for Rs 2 per bed per night) and eat at the staff canteen where the food is superb. You can also buy fresh milk, bread and cake — the only place between Kathmandu and Everest. This is a comparative oasis in the wilderness.
>
> *John Anderson, England*

**Day 5: Jiri-Thodung** (8 hours walking)
The fair-sized Newar town of Those is only a few hours walk from Jiri, it used to be famous for the extraction of iron ore and the manufacture of khukris. This is a good place to buy supplies and in spring, summer or autumn a trip to the Thodung cheese factory is a must. Thodung at 3091 m is only two hours from the main trail and you can have yak cheese and other luxuries. On the way you pass through Changma (2040 m) the first of many Sherpa villages with its typical mani walls.

> Do not miss stopping at the Thodung Cheese Factory for great cheese omelettes, fine hospitality and a cup of coffee that is out of this world. It is only an hour away from the main trail.
>
> *Robert Hanchett, USA*

**Day 6: Thodung-Sete** (6 hours walking)
A 500 m descent brings you to the Likhu Khola River followed by a 2000 m ascent to the Lamjura Pass (3530 m). That would be too much for one day so it is best to stop at the village of Sete (3575 m), still a 1000 m climb from the river.

**Day 7: Sete-Junibesi** (6 hours walking)
The Lamjura Pass will reward you with rhododendron flowers in spring and snow in the winter. From the top it is a 1000 m descent to the village of Junibesi (2675 m) which is very popular with most visitors. There is a beautiful monastery just an hour away from the main trail.

**Day 8: Junibesi-Manidingma** (6 hours walking)

A 700 m ascent takes you to the Salung Ridge; then a 500 m descent follows to the Solu Khola River. The beautiful village of Ringmo is just three hours from Junibesi and is followed by another climb to the Taksindu Pass at 3200 m. There is a monastery with guest house nearby and the view from the pass includes the mountains and the Dudh Kosi River. A descent follows to the village of Manidingma at 2316 m.

**Day 9 and 10: Manidingma-Kharekhola-Puiyan-Phakding**

The Dudh Kosi River is an 800 m descent from Manidingma, the river carries water melted from Everest itself. It is a climb once more up to the village of Khare Khola (2073 m) and then the village of Puiyan (2835 m). Lukla with its STOL field is slightly off the main trail and higher up.

**Day 11: Lukla-Namche Bazar** (5 hours walking)

From this point it is almost all up into the Sherpa country. Namche (3440 m), the "Sherpa capital", is the best known of the Sherpa villages because of the many Sherpas from around here who go on mountaineering expeditions. It is also the centre of the handicrafts

Sherpa

industry and the place where trekking permits may be checked. Saturday is the market day in Namche. The village of Kunde near Namche has a hospital built with New Zealand aid. A mica plant is being set up in Namche with Austrian assistance. A good place to stay in Namche is the *International Foot Rest.*

> **Hotel Everest View** — Kathmandu office tel 13854 — 12 rooms all with bath and view of Mt Everest — restaurant — bar — electricity — oxygen if needed — yak hire — solar heating — $US58 plus service & taxes for single, $US102 for double — STOL flight from Kathmandu $US45 — open from October to May

## Day 12: Namche-Tyangboche (5 hours walking)

The Syangboche STOL field is a short climb above Namche. Slightly higher than this is the *Everest View Hotel* which may be expensive but not only does every room have a view of Everest but you can also see it from your bathtub! From here the trail descends to meet the main Namche-Tyangboche trail and continues down to the Dudh Kosi where there is a small tea shop and a series of picturesque water-driven prayer wheels. A steep ascent brings you to the famous monastery of Tyangboche (3875 m). The monastery is totally surrounded by mountain peaks and offers a fine view of Everest and Ama Dablam. In the full moon night of the month of November the colourful Mani Rimdu festival is held here with much singing and dancing.

> The most scenic part of the Everest trek is between Tyangboche and Pangboche and it is at this altitude where the good points of trekking can really be appreciated.
>
> *Phil Martin, England*

## Day 13 and 14: Tyangboche-Pheriche-Lobuche

Beyond Tyangboche it is important to ensure that you are in good physical shape. A descent and ascent takes you to Pangboche where the monastery has a "yeti scalp". Pheriche is the last Sherpa village and has a first aid post, where there is usually a doctor, as well as offering an excellent view of Everest. There are tea shops at Lobuche (4930 m) but little shelter is available beyond this point and unless you are on an organised trek with tents it is best to use Lobuche as a base and make day treks from here. Kala Pathar (5545 m) offers the best view of Everest obtainable anywhere but the base camp (5340 m), from which the mountain is not visible, and the lake at Gorak Shep (5160 m) are also worth visiting.

**Important Note:** The number of days given here are a minimum number of walking days, it is important to be adequately rested and acclimatised.

Particularly at Namche or Tyangboche a day's rest is advisable. Remember the victims of altitude sickness are often the fittest and healthiest people who foolishly over extend themselves.

## HELAMBU TREK

If your time is limited and you cannot go far from the Kathmandu Valley the Helambu trek takes you to a Sherpa area where you can see how these fine Buddhist people differ from their lowland neighbours. The trek lasts a week or ten days and does not go above 3000 m.

The two main villages of Helambu, Tarkeghyang and Sermathan are situated at 2800 m and 2600 m respectively so you are not in really high country. It is possible to climb higher to the Gosaikund lake (4290 m) or go to the Langtang Valley through the Ganja La Pass (5106 m) but this high altitude pass is only feasible between May and September. Spectacular views of the Himalayan peaks are only to be found if you go higher on this trek but in compensation the people are friendly and hospitable and almost every Sherpa house in the region will quickly be converted to a "hotel" to welcome tourists as "paying guests".

During the Rana period the Helambu region was well known for its beautiful Sherpa girls many of whom worked for aristocratic Rana families in Kathmandu. The area has, therefore, been open to outside influence for a long time and almost everybody understands Nepali. Recently many people have gone to work on road construction in northeast India but almost all of them come back during February-March. In the summer most of the people left in the villages are either very young or very old.

In Tibetan the word Helambu means radish and potato and the area is heavily dependant on these products ; rice and wheat cannot be grown at this altitude. Large quantities of radishes and potatoes are exported to the lowlands in exchange for rice and other commodities. Apples are also grown in the Helambu area.

Helambu is a region, not a specific village. There are two ways to Helambu from Kathmandu and it is probably best to go one way and return the other. From Panchkhal on the road to the Chinese border you can follow the Melemchi River to Tarkeghyang, the most important village in the region. This route only involves two days of uphill walking whereas the alternate route from Sundarijal requires an ascent followed by two days of descent before more uphill work. The Sundarijal route does offer a good view of the mountains from Patibhanjyang and both routes meet in the village of Taran Maran before the steepest ascent. Sundarijal, at the northern end of the Kathmandu Valley, can be reached by taxi or you can bus to Bodhnath and walk there in three hours.

Trek to Helambu to see Sherpa houses, wood carved cabinets and fantastic brass and copper pots. The people will serve you rice, dal and Sherpa tea consisting of tea, ghee and salt.

*Ludi Grothelaw, Australia*

## Day 1: Panchkhal-Bahunpati (7 hours walking)

An early start from Kathmandu is essential to reach Bahunpati on the first day, the 6 am bus will get you to Panchkhal by 9 am. The trail follows the Indrawati River and involves no steep ascents or descents. Bahunpati is a small bazaar and has some government offices and a recently-constructed tourist bungalow.

## Day 2: Bahunpati-Taran Maran (4 hours walking)

You continue to follow the Indrawati River to the village of Melemchi (820 m) from where the trail follows the Melemchi River to Taran Mara at 1204 m. The trail from Sundarijal meets here and there are places to stay. The short walk allows plenty of rest before the steep climb the next day.

## Day 3: Taran Maran-Tarkeghyang

If you are a good walker you may be able to reach Tarkeghyang the same evening you start from Taran Maran. As it is a climb of almost 1800 m to the village you may not make it and may have to stop in Kiul at 1500 m, Thimpu at 1680 m or Kakani at 1850 m.

The trek to Helambu offers alternative routes of three to four days and friendly homes for overnight stays along most of the way. Individual farms and homes are preferable especially in Tarkeghyang which has a landing pad for helicopter tourists and a noticeably higher standard of living.

*Ron Bitzer, USA*

## Day 4: Tarkeghyang-Sermathan (4 hours walking)

A French student once told me that Tarkeghyang resembled a village in the alps, you'll reach it on the fourth day if not before. There is a festival in the village on the full moon in March with a feast in the evening and a mask dance followed by dancing till midnight. The ceremony takes place in a new monastery. The houses are clustered together in Tarkeghyang in contrast to the next village of Sermathan, only three to four hours walk away with no steep ascents or descents. Sermathan is at an altitude of 2600 m and the trail runs through a beautiful forest. Less commercialised than Tarkeghyang, Sermathan is also an important apple growing area and has a government horticulture farm. Although the mountains visible are not particularly notable the view is scenic and the beautiful natural setting also gives a good view of the valley of the Melemchi River to the south.

# Booklist

An amazing number of books have been written about exploring Nepal, mountaineering in Nepal and on its culture, art, religions and architecture. The list that follows is simply a selection of some of the more interesting books. Some of them may only be readily available in Nepal, others are long out of print and may only be found in libraries.

## GENERAL

*The Wildest Dreams of Kew* Jeremy Bernstein, Simon and Schuster, New York, 1970 – a very readable account of Nepal's history and an evocative description of the trek to the Everest base camp.

*Nepal – the Kingdom in the Himalayas* Toni Hagen, Kummerley and Frey, Berne, 1961 – the definitive record of the geology and people of Nepal by the same man who, until the early sixties, had probably seen more of the country than anyone else – westerner or Nepali. Many interesting personal insights makes it particularly interesting and some excellent colour photography.

*Mustang – a Lost Tibetan Kingdom* Michel Peissel, Collins and Harvill Press, 1968 – a somewhat over excited description of a visit to the isolated region of Mustang north of the Annapurnas and close to the Tibetan border.

*Nepal Namaste* Robert Rieffel, Sahayogi Prakashan, Kathmandu, 1975 – a good general guidebook to Nepal.

*Katmandu* Colin Simpson, Angus and Robertson, Sydney, 1967 – an attractive book on a visit to Kathmandu and Pokhara, with some fine photographs.

*The Mountain is Young* Han Suyin, Jonathan Cape, London, 1971 – a flowery women's magazine style fictional romance set in Nepal in the mid-fifties.

## CULTURE, PEOPLES, FESTIVALS

*Festivals of Nepal* Mary Anderson, George Allen and Unwin, London, 1971 – covers the many festivals celebrated in Nepal.

*People of Nepal* Dor Bahadur Bista, Ratna Pustak Bhandar, Kathmandu – deals in detail with the different ethnic groups of Nepal.

*Sherpas of Nepal* C Von Furer-Haimendorf, John Murray, London 1964 – a rather dry study of the Sherpas of the Everest region.

*Tigers for Breakfast* Michel Peissel, Hodder and Stoughton, London, 1966 – a biography of the well known Boris Lissanevith of the Royal Hotel and Yak and Yeti Restaurant.

*The Gods of Nepal* Mary Rubel, Shivaratna Harsharatna, Kathmandu, 1968 – a detailed description of the Hindu and Buddhist deities.

## ART AND ARCHITECTURE

*Kathmandu Valley Towns* Fran Hosken, Weatherhill, New York, 1974 – more than 500 colour and black and white photographs of the towns, temples and people of the valley and an introduction to its history and festivals.

*Himalayan Art* Madanjeet Sing, Macmillan, London, 1968 – an introduction to the art of the whole Himalayan region with beautiful picture.

*An Introduction to the Hanuman Dhoka* Institute of Nepal and Asian Studies, Kirtipur, 1975 — an excellent description of the old Royal Palace and the many buildings clustered in Kathmandu's Durbar Square.

## TREKKING

*Trekking in the Himalayas* Stan Armington, Lonely Planet, Melbourne, 1976 — everything you need to know before setting out for a trek in Nepal.

*A Guide to Trekking in Nepal* Stephen Bezruchka, Sahayogi Press, Kathmandu, 1974 — a detailed description of the main trekking routes for the independent trekker.

*Sherpa, Himalaya, Nepal* Mario Fantin — good photographs and a detailed description of the Everest trek and the sherpas of that region.

*Trekking in Mt Everest and Solu Khumbu, Trekking North of Pokhara* and *Helambu, Langtang Valley and Ganja la* John L Hayes, Peter Purna Books, Kathmandu, 1976 — This series of trekking guides gives a detailed description of each of the above treks and even an altitude profile.

*A Winter in Nepal* John Morris, Rupert Hart-Davis, London, 1964 — a very readable account of a Kathmandu to Pokhara trek by a retired British army Gurkha officer whose fluent Nepali allowed him to make some interesting observations of Nepalese life.

*Nepal Himalaya* H W Tillman, Cambridge University Press, London, 1952 — if you can find this book in libraries, it gives a fascinating account of some easy going rambles around Nepal by an Everest pioneer of the thirties together with some astonishingly unplanned (by today's standards) mountain assaults.

## MOUNTAINS & MOUNTAINEERING

*Annapurna South Face* Chris Bonnington, Cassell, London, 1971 — an interesting account of the new highly technical assaults on difficult mountain faces plus the problems of expedition organisation and the sheer logistics of carrying out the climb.

*Everest the Hard Way* Chris Bonnington, Hodder and Stoughton, London, 1976 (also available in paperback) — the exciting story of the perfectly timed and executed rush to the summit in 1975, the first successful ascent by the south-west face. Backed up by some of the most amazing mountaineering photographs ever taken.

*Everest South-West Face* Chris Bonnington, Hodder and Stoughton, London, 1973 — an account of the author's earlier, and unsuccessful, attempt on the most difficult Everest face.

*To the Third Pole* G O Dhyrenfurth, Munich, 1960 — the post war attacks on the world's highest peaks, the third pole of the world according to this expedition leader.

*Annapurna* Maurice Herzog, Jonathan Cape, London, 1952 — a classic description of the first successful conquest of an 8,000 metre peak and the harrowing, frostbitten aftermath.

*The Conquest of Everest* Sir John Hunt, Hodder and Stoughton, London, 1953 — the first successful climb of the world's highest mountain.

*Annapurna to Dhaulagiri* Dr Harka Gurung, Department of Information, HMG, Kathmandu — describes the mountaineering activity in Nepal between 1950 and 1960 when almost all the major peaks were conquered.

*The Himalayas — a Journey to Nepal* Takehide Kazami, Kodanshi International, 1968 — one of the Japanese "This Beautiful World" series with stunningly beautiful colour photographs of many of Nepal's peaks.

*Himalaya* Herbert Tichy, Robert Hale, London, 1970 — a chatty series of incidents and anecdotes from the authors Himalayan wanderings since the thirties, including the ascent of Cho Oyu, at the time the third highest peak climbed.

---

## Hashish

One of the reasons for the increasing popularity of Kathmandu in the late sixties and early seventies, particularly amongst the *freak* community, was the unlimited availability of hashish and even stronger drugs. Although the smoking of hashish had been free in Nepal until 1973 few local people smoked it apart from the *sadhus* or holy men. Some young Nepalese were starting to smoke as a result of association with freaks however. Hash smoking is now supposed to be banned but people say it still goes on. Taking hash out of the country is strictly prohibited and several people have been arrested at the airport trying to smuggle it out. A recent study conducted by the government showed that many areas in the hills of western Nepal where people had been dependent on the cultivation of marijuana had been adversely effected by the ban.

# Glossary

**Apron** — colourful aprons are worn by all married Tibetan women.

**Ashoka** — Indian emperor who did much to spread Buddhism 2500 years ago, including to Nepal.

**Asla** — river trout.

**Avalokitesvara** — Hindu/Buddhist god whose incarnation is Machhendranath.

**Bakba** — Tibetan clay mask.

**Bajra** — see Dorje.

**Bazar** — market area, a market town is called a bazar.

**Bel Tree** — young Newari girls are symbolically "wed" to a bel tree to ensure that the death of any .future husband does not leave them a widow.

**Bhairab** — the fearful manifestation of Shiva.

**Bhati** — tea shop/rest house in western Nepal.

**Bon Po** — the animist pre-Buddhist religion of Tibet.

**Brahmins** — the priestly caste of Hindus who also form one of Nepal's major ethnic groups.

**Chakra** — disc-like weapon of Vishnu.

**Chang** — Tibetan rice beer.

**Chappati** — unleavened Indian bread.

**Chautara** — stone platforms built around trees along walking trails as resting places for walkers.

**Chetris** — prince and warrior caste of Hindus, the present king and all the Ranas were chetris.

**China Lama** — the chief lama at Bodhnath.

**Chomolongma** — Tibetan name for Mt Everest, '' Mother Goddess of the World''.

**Chortens** — Tibetan Buddhist stupas.

**Chowk** — courtyard or market place, as Kumari Chowk (house of the living goddess) or Indrachowk (market area of Kathmandu).

**Chuba** — long woolen coats worn by Sherpas.

**Crow** — the messenger of Yama.

**Curd** — yoghurt, a speciality of Bhaktapur.

**Dal** — lentil soup that forms part of the Nepali staple diet.

**Deval** — Nepali word for temple

**Devanagari** — Nepali script, identical to Hindi and Sanskrit.

**Dhwaja** — metal plate ribbon leading up to the roof of a temple as the pathway for the gods.

**Dorje** — "thunderbolt" symbol of Buddhist power.

**Durbar** — palace, the main valley towns each have a Durbar Square, the square in front of the palace.

**Durga** — terrible manifestation of Parvati, can often be seen killing a demon in the form of a buffalo.

**Earthquakes** — are rare in Nepal but major ones shook the valley in 1833 and 1934.

**Everest** — the highest mountain in the world, named after George Everest, the British Surveyor General of India at the time the British discovered it.

**Flag** — Nepal is the only country in the world which does not have a rectangular flag.

**Freaks** — the young westerners who wander the east and can be found congregating in Bali, Kabul, Goa and Kathmandu.

**Gaines** — beggar minstrels.
**Ganesh** — elephant-headed son of Shiva and Parvati.
**Ganja** — hashish.
**Garuda** — man-bird vehicle of Vishnu, often found kneeling before shrines to Vishnu — human like except for wings.
**Ghee** — clarified butter.
**Ghat** — steps down to a river, bodies are cremated on a "burning ghat".
**Gompa** — Tibetan Buddhist monastery.
**Gopis** — cow herd girls, Shiva is said to have dallied with them on the river banks at Pashupatinath.
**Gurkha** — originally derived from the name of the region of Gorkha, it came to be used for all soldiers recruited from Nepal for the British army.
**Gurkhali** — another name for the language Nepali.
**Gurr** — a baked, grated potato dish prepared by the Sherpas. •
**Gurungs** — people from the western hill regions, particularly around Gorkha and Annapurna.

**Hanuman** — Monkey God.
**Hashish** — dried resin from the marijuana plant.

**Indra** — King of the Vedic Gods.

**Kali Gandaki** — between Annapurna and Dhaulagiri this river cuts the deepest gorge in the world.
**Kali** — terrifying manifestation of Goddess.
**Kartikiya** — God of War and son of Shiva.
**Kata** — Tibetan prayer shawl, traditionally given to a lama when one is brought to his presence.

**Khukri** — curved, traditional knife of the Nepalese, used with devasting ability by the Gurkhas.
**Kinkinimali** — temple wind bells.
**Krishna** — the eighth incarnation of Vishnu, often coloured blue.
**Kumari** — more peaceful incarnation of Kali. The Nepali name of the living goddess in Kathmandu is also Kumari.

**Lama** — Tibetan Buddhist priest or holy man, also respectful name.
**Laxmi** — Goddess of Wealth, consort of Vishnu.
**Leeches** — unpleasant blood-sucking creatures that appear in great numbers along the trekking trails during the monsoon — to get rid of them use a lighted cigarette, salt or insect spray, but do not try to pull them off.
**Lingam** — phallically shaped symbol of Shiva's creative powers.

**Machendranath** — patron God of the Kathmandu Valley.
**Mahabharata** — ancient Hindu epic.
**Mahseer** — giant game fish caught in the rivers of the Terai.
**Malla** — dynasty which ruled the valley from the 13th to the 18th century and created some of the finest art and architecture in the valley.
**Mandala** — geometrical and astrological representation of the world.
**Mandir** — Nepalese word for temple.
**Manjushree** — God who cut the Chobar Gorge and drained the dammed-up waters from the valley.
**Mani Stone** — stone carved with the Buddhist chant "Om mani padne hum" — oh you jewel in the lotus.
**Mani Wall** — wall built of these stones in the hill country, always walk by one with the wall on your right.
**Mantra** — prayer formula or chant.
**Mara** — Buddhist God of Death, has three eyes and holds the wheel of life.

**Mirror** — usually found on temples to help devotees place their tikas.

**Monsoon** — rainy period from mid-June to late-September when there is rainfull virtually every day; there is also a very short winter monsoon, lasting a day or two usually in late January.

**Muktinah** — holy place north of Pokhara where a natural gas flame and water issue from the same rock.

**Naga** — serpent deity.

**Namaste** — Nepalese greeting.

**Names** — male Sherpas are named after the day of the week they were born: Monday — Dawa, Tuesday — Mingma, Wednesday — Lakpa, Thursday — Phurbu, Friday — Pasang, Saturday — Pemba, Sunday — Nyima.

**Nandi** — the bull, animal of Shiva.

**Narayan** — incarnation of Vishnu.

**Narsimha (Narsingha)** — man-lion incarnation of Vishnu.

**Newars** — original people of the Kathmandu Valley who were responsible for the architectural style of the valley.

**Nilakantha** — form of Shiva with blue throat caused by swallowing poison that would have ruined the world.

**Oriflammes** — prayer flags, prayers written on them are carried off by the breeze.

**Pagoda** — multi-storied Nepalese temple, this style originated in Nepal and was later taken up in China and Japan.

**Panchayat** — village democracy, the partyless government of Nepal.

**Pashupati** — incarnation of Shiva.

**Patakas** — see dhwajas.

**Porters** — hill people who carry goods along the trails of roadless Nepal.

**Prashad** — consecrated food.

**Prayer Wheels** — cylindrical wheel inscribed with a Buddhist prayer which devotees spin round, in the hill country there are water-driven prayer wheels.

**Puja** — religious ritual or observance.

**Raksi** — rice spirit.

**Ramayana** — Hindu epic telling of the adventures of Prince Rama and his beautiful wife Sita and the demon King Ravana.

**Rana** — the series of hereditary Prime Ministers who ruled Nepal from 1846 to 1951.

**Refugees** — thousands of refugees fled to Nepal from Tibet after the Chinese invasion.

**Reincarnate Lama** — lama who has been selected for his position due to indications that he is the reincarnated form of a previous lama.

**Rhododendrons** — in Nepal rhododendrons are not a small decorative bush but a huge, brilliant tree which blooms in March and April above 2000 metres.

**Ropeway** — built from Thankot in the valley to Dharsing in 1929, to bring goods up from India, still in use today.

**Sagarmatha** — Nepalese name for Mt Everest.

**Sankha** — conch shell symbol of Vishnu.

**Sarangi** — violins played by the gaines.

**Sherpas** — hill people of eastern Nepal who became famous from their exploits with mountaineering expeditions, literally means "people from the east".

**Sherpanis** — female Sherpas.

**Shivaratri** — birthday of Shiva.

**Sirdar** — leader/organiser of a group of porters.

**Solu Khumbu** — Everest region of eastern Nepal where the majority of the Sherpas live.

**Sonam** — kharma built up during successive incarnations.

**STOL** — short take-off and landing aircraft.

**Stupa** — Buddhist religious structure like a circular mound surmounted by a spire, always walk around stupas clockwise.

### Mahabouddha

**Shikara** — Indian style temple like Krishna Mandir or Mahabouddha temple in Patan.

**Tanka** — rectangular Tibetan paintings on cotton, framed with brocade strips.

**Tantra** — symbolic and metaphysical religious philosophy evolved in the 10th to 15th century that binds Hindu and Buddhist people in Nepal.

**Tempos** — small three-wheeled transports commonly used in Kathmandu — similar to Thai samlors or Balinese bemos.

**Terai** — flat land of southern Nepal.

**Thakalis** — people of western Nepal around Jomosom who specialise in running hotels and bhatis.

**Tika** — red sandal wood paste spot marked on the forehead as a religious mark and on women as an indication of marriage.

**Tribhuvan** — grandfather of the present king who ended the period of Rana rule in 1951, the road to the Indian border from Kathmandu and the Kathmandu airport are named after him.

**Trisul** — trident weapon of Shiva.

**Topi** — traditional Nepalese cap.

**Torana** — ornament above temple doors which indicate to which God the temple is dedicated.

**Tsampa** — barley flour porridge of the Sherpas.

**Valley** — until fairly recently the Kathmandu Valley was almost synonymous with Nepal, the country is still a conglomeration of many different peoples and ethnic groups.

**Vihar** — religious buildings comprising sanctuaries and lodgings for pilgrims.

**Vishnu** — the preserver, has many incarnations in Nepal.

**Yak** — main beast of burden and form of cattle in the high country above 3000 metres.

**Yama** — God of Death.

**Yeti** — the abominable snowman.

**Yoni** — female sexual symbol usually found with lingams.

**Zhum** — female offspring of a yak and a cow.

# Index

To watch a sunset, preferably alone near the temple on the river, and see a Nepalese day end is an experience both interesting and educational. You see the water buffaloes washed, the goats being driven home and the sun fade away behind the mountains with Swayambhu in the distance.

*Suzi Albright, USA*